THE SCIENCE OF ECONOMICS

Edited by Fred Foldvary
Santa Clara University

cognella
San Diego, CA

First published in the United States of America in 2011 by Cognella, a division of University Readers, Inc.

15 14 13 12 11 1 2 3 4 5

Printed in the United States of America

ISBN: 978-1-609279-40-0

cognella™

www.cognella.com 800.200.3908

Contents

Chapter 1: The Foundations of Economic Theory

A. THE QUEST FOR ECONOMIC PROSPERITY WITH JUSTICE

The most important reason for learning economics is to understand social reality. Things are not what they appear to be. There is often an implicit reality that is not visible, obvious, or apparent. We need economic understanding to be able to know the reality. Economics enables us to understand the implicit reality beneath the superficial appearances of economic activity.

Many people also study economics because they wish to understand why we have social problems such as unemployment and poverty, and how these problems can be remedied. Most people have similar visions of prosperity and justice. We want to live in social harmony, where everyone who wants to can work and make a good living. We would like to eliminate poverty and live in a healthy environment.

We can envision ideal worlds, but they must be founded on sound principles if our vision is to succeed. Too often, as was the case with totalitarian central planning, utopian dreams turn into horrific nightmares because they have been based on unsound premises. This book presents a "paradigm" or basic analysis of economics called "foundational economics," which will enable you to understand the major social issues of our time and, as importantly, to be able to analyze assertions made by people, including politicians and economic authorities, to determine whether they are sound or contain incomplete theories or outright fallacies. The primary aim of this book is to enable you to think for yourself and analyze economic issues in a fundamental, logical, scientific way. The only authorities in economics, as in any science, are logic and evidence. The only prerequisite or prior knowledge needed is an open but critical mind.

The basic principle of foundational economics, the paradigm analyzed in this book, is that the market economy works, providing efficiency, equity, and sustainability. The legal structure and the government fiscal or tax policy must be in harmony with economic and ethical principles for it to work properly.

B. THE CONCEPT OF AN ECONOMIC MODEL

A model boat is a small-scale replica of the larger real-world item. A fashion model demonstrates clothes which real-world people could wear. A map is a model of some physical territory. Science also has models. Like the boat, it is similar to the object being analyzed, but smaller in the sense of being simpler and more abstract. Real-world people are usually not as beautiful or slender as models, but the model still shows how the clothes would be worn. A scientific model is a set of concepts and propositions which, like maps, demonstrate the main features of the phenomenon being analyzed. Often a model will have some very restrictive premises that simplify the phenomenon in order to emphasize a few of its aspects (for example, ignoring friction in a physics model to focus on gravity), and these premises are later relaxed (friction is then added) to bring in some realistic complications after some conclusions have been made about the main features.

For example, the story of Robinson Crusoe alone in an island is a favorite model that illustrates some economic concepts concerning only one individual; then, the second person, Friday, can be brought in to complicate things and make it closer to real-world experience. A large amount of theory is explained with such models.

Many economic models consist of premises from which conclusions are logically deduced. If the premises are general, they constitute pure theory, often conditional on certain non-universal secondary premises. If the premises include data from history or current economic figures, they become specific theories, whether descriptive or predictive. Many economic models are mathematical, with premises consisting of algebraic variables, functions and equations, the deduction being mainly mathematical manipulation. Many economic models can be "quantified" and tested by statistical or "econometric" calculations using computers. Computer programs have also been used as models that simulate economies. However, such programming, statistical analysis and higher math (which is avoided in this book) is not really needed to understand the basic concepts and theories of economics.

C. POSITIVE AND NORMATIVE ECONOMICS

"Positive" economics is the study of the actual phenomena of the world, including predictions about the future. "Normative" economics concerns what one thinks economic policy should be, or how an economy is best established. It judges economies or some economic process by some norm or moral standard, or by some standard of efficiency.

People, including economists and politicians, often make normative statements based on their personal values or the values of some group. But if values are all personal and arbitrary, then is it possible to have a scientific theory of normative economics? This would require a scientific, or non-arbitrary, moral standard. Such a universal ethic has been derived in my book *The Soul of Liberty* (1980). What is not so evident is that a rational ethic is important not only for policy, but for an understanding of a market economy as well. This concept is explained in the following section.

D. THE ETHICAL FOUNDATION OF A MARKET ECONOMY

It is not enough to say that a market consists of voluntary acts, since we can then ask, what exactly are such acts? If your better product leaves me with fewer profits, that competition would not likely have my consent, yet it is not considered to be involuntary. So we need some ethical rules to tell which acts are voluntary; indeed, to define the concept of "voluntary."

In the discussion of normative economics above, the possibility of a universal ethic, a moral standard that does not depend on any particular culture or personal view, was raised. The full treatment of this ethic is beyond the scope of this book; interested readers are referred to *The Soul of Liberty*, as mentioned above. A brief outline of the derivation is useful, however, so that the ethic is not simply presented as fiat.

The two premises of the universal ethic were recognized by the philosopher John Locke (1690): independence and equality. Each human being thinks and acts as an internally independent living being, although he is socially dependent on others. As a common species, the qualities that make us reasoning beings with the capacity of deliberate choice is equal to all. These premises are based on human nature, hence the ethic derived from these premises is referred to as "natural moral law" or, if the context is clear, just "natural law."

As an independent mind, each person perceives that the acts of others are either pleasing or displeasing to oneself, hence they are personally and subjectively good or bad. All values originate in these individual valuations. Therefore, no act can be universally deemed as good unless the recipient of the act deems it as good, and if he considers it good, one may not declare that it is universally not good, since the recipient is a moral equal. Hence, acts that benefit others must be considered good by the universal ethic.

Similarly, an act which affects no other person cannot be designated as evil if the person doing it does not consider it evil. Such acts can be generally designated as neutral, neither good nor evil.

This leaves us with acts which affect others negatively. Let's divide them into two categories, those which depend only on the state of the recipient's mind, which will be called "offenses," and those, called "harms," which do not. For example, if X objects to Y's religious views, this depends only on the personal views of X. On the other hand, if Y stabs X with a knife, this injury does not depend only on X's beliefs; it is an invasion, an unwelcome entering from outside of X into the domain of X.

Harms are considered bad or evil by the recipient, and thus also designated as evil by the universal ethic, since the only source of values is the individual. But offenses cannot be designated as evil, since the universal ethic, as noted above, is by definition independent of personal views; if the injury is caused only by such a subjective view, then the universal ethic designates it as neutral. We then have two definitions and three rules that make up the universal ethic:

A benefit is an act the recipient deems to be pleasing.

A harm is a direct, actual, invasive injury.

1. Acts that benefit others are good.
2. Acts that coercively harm others are evil.
3. All other acts are neutral, neither good nor evil.

A "voluntary" act can now be defined as one which is not evil according to the universal ethic. The totality of such acts in a certain context constitutes a market in the broadest sense.

With this universal ethic we can now derive natural or human rights, and the concept of "liberty." Liberty is defined as the absence of any legal restrictions on human action, other than those prohibiting and penalizing coercive harm. Moral rights are just another way of stating what is morally wrong. Natural rights are moral rights based on the moral law expressed by the universal ethic. If you have a moral right to do or have something, it means that it is wrong for others to prevent you from doing or having it.

Since economic resources boil down to land and labor, rights to either are fundamental. Since any arbitrary restriction on human action is invasive, a person has self-ownership, including the right to labor without restrictions other than against force and fraud. Since one has a right to one's time and energy, hence labor, one has a right to the reward of the labor, or wages. One also then has a right to the product of labor, produced wealth or capital goods. The taxation of labor or capital is therefore a violation of natural rights.

Land is a product of nature, not human exertion, so self-ownership does not apply to natural resources. Here, the equality premise applies: the right to the benefits of natural resources prior to their alteration by human effort belongs equally to all in the relevant community. As will be analyzed below, the efficient economic implementation of equal benefits is not a physical division of land, nor necessarily a community control over it, but by the collection of its rent to fund community services, leaving possession in individual hands.

This ethic is implemented by a body of law. The most fundamental and supreme set of laws, from which all other laws derive their authority, is a "constitution." The constitution of a community having a free society and free markets needs to determine the rules for property rights, the resolution of disputes, and the laws concerning contracts. A constitution is what economist James Buchanan (1987, p. 58) called a "choice of constraints" in contrast to a choice within constraints.

E. THE MEANING AND METHODOLOGY OF ECONOMICS

The first aspect of methodology is careful definition. The key words of the field need to be concisely and precisely defined, so that the meaning in that context is clear.

"Economics" has been defined in several ways. The classical definition is that economics is the social science dealing with real wealth. Wealth, in the economic sense, is not money (which has value as generally exchangeable for real wealth), but thegoods which people produce. Thus, economics is a social science, dealing with the activities of people, and it specializes in the production, distribution, exchange, and consumption of wealth, or the material needs and desires of human beings.

But wealth is not an end in itself. People desire goods for the use, enjoyment, and value that they generate. These qualities as a whole are labeled "utility" in economics. Leisure time also has utility, and economics also takes into account the choice of not producing something but rather enjoying free time instead. Therefore, a broader and deeper definition of the subject is: economics is the science of utility. In contrast, related social sciences can be characterized as follows. Political science is the study of governance; sociology is the study of relationships; psychology is the study of genetically caused behavior; and anthropology is the study of human evolution and culture. These related fields impact on utility, and so are interdependent with economics.

In producing and consuming wealth, or pursuing utility, people do not behave randomly. As the Austrian economist Ludwig von Mises (1949, p. 4) stated, "Human action is purposeful behavior." People tend to follow particular laws or regularities due to their human nature. "The ultimate goal of human action is always the satisfaction of the acting man's desire" (p. 14). These desires, and the values people place on things, are subjective. People choose among alternatives, which implies they are able to rank their desires into those of greater and lessor importance.

It is also a fundamental fact that the resources from which wealth is produced are scarce. Some economists, following Lionel Robbins (1932) have therefore defined economics as "the allocation of scarce resources among alternative uses in order to satisfy human desires." This is descriptive of what goes on, but it seems less than comprehensive and yet overly detailed for a foundational definition of the scientific field, like saying that physics is "the examination of space, particles, energy, and time in the determination of laws and measurements of the fundamental phenomena of the universe" instead of the simpler but comprehensive meaning, "the science of fundamental universal phenomena." Hence, in my judgment, a more parsimonious yet comprehensive definition of economics is "the science of utility."

The "methodology" of a science is the methods, techniques, and scientific philosophy used in obtaining knowledge. The methodology presented in this book is "foundational." The basic principles of foundational economics include definitions of key terms, the "taxonomy" or division of a field into meaningful categories, the formulation of premises universal to the field, the deduction of pure theory by the use of logic, the discovery of empirical knowledge by observation, the realization that our perceptions are tinged by our interpretations, and the discovery of specific theories regarding events and particular people, areas, and histories with conjectures and hypotheses tested by data.

In economics as in any science, the only authorities are logic and evidence, not the views and sayings of any person as such. As Henry George (1883, p. 242) stated it, "I ask no one who may read this book to accept my views. I ask him to think for himself."

F. THE FOUNDATIONAL PREMISES OF ECONOMICS

After defining key terms, a field of science requires fundamental premises or first principles. These are propositions or statements that apply to the whole universe of the field; in social science, this means they are valid for all people, in all times, places, and cultures. The following universal propositions are foundational for economics:

Propositions about physical resources and technology

1. Some natural resources are scarce relative to human desires.
2. Resources vary in quality.
3. After some level of use, given the existence of one of more fixed resources, the use of extra amounts of a variable resource will produce ever smaller extra amounts of output (the law of diminishing returns).
4. Different amounts and methods of production may produce different amounts of output for the same proportion of inputs, i.e. returns to scale and to techniques can vary.

Propositions about human biology

5. All human beings belong to the same species and have the same human nature.

6. The human lifetime is finite.
7. Human beings have children who need care, and in old age, may no longer be able to work.

Propositions about human behavior and thought

8. Human beings have ends, i.e. goals, desires, and needs.
9. Human beings are able to rank their ends, i.e. into those of greater and lesser importance.
10. Human desires tend to be unlimited.
11. Human values, both moral and material, are subjective.
12. Human beings economize: they desire to obtain things with the least possible unpleasant exertion, or equivalently, with some level of exertion, to obtain as much as possible.
13. The desires and motivations of human beings include 1) self-interest, ends connected with their own survival, happiness, and power, and 2) the well being of those for whom they have sympathy.
14. People tend to have a "time preference," preferring goods at present to those in the future.

Proposition about the future

15. The future is uncertain.

The tenth proposition was noted by Henry George, who stated (1879, p. 507) that desires "short of infinity can never be satisfied," and (1883, p. 33) that "Man is not like the ox. He has no fixed standard of satisfaction." George (1879, p. 204) also stated the twelfth premise as a "fundamental principle of human action" that "men seek to gratify their desires with the least exertion." Carl Menger (1871, pp. 95–6) defined the principle of "economizing" thus: "men endeavor ... to obtain the greatest possible result with a given quantity of a good or a given result with the smallest possible quantity."

These universal propositions are warranted by empirical observation and logic; most of them are obvious. We can observe that these phenomenon occur and that they are not limited to any particular time, place, or culture. This inductive analysis involves a subjective investigation of one's own behavior and sentiments as well as the observation of the acts of others (which we interpret also from a knowledge of our own interior motives).

From these universal propositions or premises, the next element of economic methodology is to logically deduce propositions which make up "pure theory," pure because this theory applies universally. "Theory" is a systematically organized collection or set of propositions, a "theorem" being a proposition or statement that is warranted by logic and evidence. Some of these conclusions or statements may be conditional, depending on secondary premises which may or may not be applicable to a particular time or place.

G. DEDUCTIVE AND INDUCTIVE THEORY

As stated above, the 15 foundational propositions are based on empirical observations which any person may verify for oneself from experience. Empirical or factual observations are then also used to verify deduced theories, to test whether the logic is sound.(It should be noted, however, that induction itself is also a type of deduction, since it involves two sets of premises: 1) a collection of observed facts; 2) rules by which one generalizes from facts. Deductions are then made using the data and rules.)

Using pure theory, economists then obtain knowledge about specific phenomena, events, and regularities that do pertain to some culture, time, or place. In physical and life science, scientists can perform experiments, while in social science, we rely mainly on the evidence from history, although economists also conduct experiments (often with students as subjects).

The method of finding specific theory is called "hypothetical deductive." An economist uses principles of pure theory to make an educated guess about some specific phenomenon; this is called a "hypothesis." The hypothesis is then tested with evidence, usually from current practices, from present and past data, or historical documents. If the evidence contradicts the hypothesis, the hypothesis is rejected. If the evidence is consistent with the hypothesis, then perhaps other tests will be conducted, and other economists will then study the results. If the tests seems sound, then the hypothesis becomes a "specific theory" about a particular phenomenon rather than a statement that is universally true. Such theory is subject to change and challenge. Pure theory is also subject to challenge, but this would be a much more fundamental and less common challenge.

An example of a specific theory is the explanation of the Great Depression, and an example of conditional specific theory is the effect on future inflation when the Federal Reserve increases the money supply, if there is no change in the velocity or turnover of money.

An important principle of all theory is that of "interpretive understanding." When we observe a phenomenon, like a wild duck or a person sawing a board, the facts do not simply speak for themselves. We do not see just the facts, but interpret them according to our previous ideas, beliefs, and values. Some people will see a wild duck and think of how good it would taste or what fun it would be to hunt; others might see a beautiful living being, part of our natural heritage that should be preserved.

When it comes to observing human action, we interpret the internal as well as external acts. The internal state of the actor includes how it thinks and feels; since we are human, we presume that other human beings act similarly to how we act. So we can imagine ourselves sawing the board, and interpret why the person would do it; perhaps he is building something. We can imagine people acting out of hunger, the desire for wealth or power, erotic stimulation, or from love and devotion. We understand these things, or think we do, because we interpret the acts from our own experience, emotions, and reasoning. But interpretations, whether of acts, art, or some text, also requires logic to make sure we on the right track. It helps to have dialogue with others about the phenomenon, to make sure we are not overly reflecting our own personal biases. That is why an important part of any science is letting others see and criticize our work.

H. THE FACTORS OF PRODUCTION

Like in the Bible, let us start our economics with the creation of the universe. In the beginning, there was the universe, and the earth. Then came human beings. As indicated above, economics is a social science, which means a science about persons. We separate the universe into human beings and "nature," defined here as everything prior to being affected by human beings. Since humans use nature to satisfy their needs and desires, nature becomes natural resources.

Things of general value that people create from nature are termed "economic wealth." This consists of things that others would value enough to be willing to offer something else in exchange. In other words, economic wealth has a market value, or value to others. Money is not economic wealth, because people do not want it for itself alone, but for the things it will buy. The term "financial wealth" is used for things with market value in general, including money, bonds, and other items that do not have intrinsic value (value due to their being wanted for their actual use). The term "wealth" can refer to either financial or economic wealth. Here, the term "wealth" will be used as a shorter synonym for economic wealth.

Since economic wealth is neither natural resources nor people, it forms a third category of economic elements, capital goods. This leaves things that people have produced, but which do not have social or market value, such as garbage. This we will call "valueless products."

"Land" is usually thought of as the solid surface of the earth. But economic land has a wider meaning, namely, all natural resources, including the waters, air, and underground resources. Here, "land" will be used as a short synonym for economic land. So, the universe is divided into land, human beings, wealth, and valueless products.

Human beings exert effort in order to produce wealth, and this time and energy is termed "labor." Labor includes all human exertion in the production of wealth, including that done by managers and entrepreneurs. Labor includes the education, skills, and training that makes workers more productive; these enhancements are called "human capital."

People also use produced goods, or tools, to produce wealth. Capital goods are wealth items which have been produced, but not yet consumed. Money or other financial instruments that are owned by a business and eventually get exchanged for wealth are called "financial capital." So the term "capital" can mean financial capital or capital goods.

These are the three "factors" or resource inputs of production. Wealth is produced using land, labor, and capital goods. This wealth is distributed or assigned to the owners of these factors, or to those who have property rights to the income of yields of the factors. Owners of land receive land rent, owners of labor (as self-owners) get wages, and the owners of capital goods get a capital yield.

Note that "wages" include any earning from wages, whether it be in the form of a salary, commission, fee, or in-kind yield, such as the fish people catch or fruit they pick. Also, much income is due to two or three factors. A farmer who owns his land earns wages from his own labor, rent from the portion of produce due to the benefit of land, and a yield on his capital goods investments, such as machines, buildings, and irrigation canals. These are income even if you pay them to yourself.

Having examined the foundations of economic theory, we will in the following chapters analyze these factors in more detail and then see how they and their products and the organization of production operate in an economy.

Chapter 2:
Labor and its Wages

1. LABOR AS A FACTOR OF PRODUCTION

This and the following two chapters will analyze the three factors of production: labor, land, and capital goods. Some people prefer the listing and analysis to be in the order of land, labor, and capital goods, for the reason that land appeared prior to human beings or is logically prior. But to understand the economics of land, we must first delve into that of labor, since the rent of land depends on the productivity of labor, hence labor is treated here first.

(This book was originally written for use by followers of Henry George, and thus much if is based on and cites the thought of this American economist,)

Henry George (1879, p. 32) provided a concise yet comprehensive definition of labor and wages: "the term labor includes all human exertion in the production of wealth, and wages, being that part of the produce which goes to labor, includes all reward for such exertion." This exertion includes both mental and physical effort, and it encompasses the efforts of entrepreneurs, managers, and the self-employed. (The Austrian economist Carl Menger (1871, p. 172) noted that "Entrepreneurial activity must definitely be counted as a category of labor services.") "Wages" includes any return or yield to labor, whether it be a salary, commission, or the profit of the self-employed. Part of the value of crops grown by a farmer on his or her own property or the gold panned by a prospector are wages.

To be meaningful, the concept of labor must be distinct from capital goods and land. George (p. 39) noted that people often speak of a worker's skill and knowledge as being "capital"; economists call these "human capital." But this meaning of "capital," he noted, is "a metaphorical use of language," and not to be confused with the use of "capital" as a resource or factor of production. A human being is different from a machine or a horse; persons are the subjects, not objects, of social science. One may consider all inputs into a productive process as "capital," but then one would still distinguish among the meaningful categories of such capital, one of which would be labor, distinct from natural resources and capital goods.

2. THE DETERMINATION OF THE WAGE LEVEL

But how does the wage level get established in the first place. And how does one account for poverty? As Henry George (p. 205) pointed out, a free man would not agree to work for another for less than he could secure by working for himself. So wages are determined by what one could earn from self-employment elsewhere. But where?

A) Wages from the product of labor

The determination of the wages of different types of labor is the result of the supply and demand for that type and quality of labor. In a pure market economy, wages ultimately reflect the value put on a worker's product by consumers: if consumers put a low value on his product then his wages will be low; if it puts no value on them, then his wages will be nil, and he will have to switch to producing a product other people want. As George (p. 77) put it, "The demand for consumption determines the direction in which labor will be expended in production."

Wages vary among different occupations because what some workers have to offer is valued more highly than what others have to offer. In consideration of one particular kind of labor, if there exists a shortage of labor then through the action of supply and demand wages for that labor will tend to rise. Conversely, where a particular labor is in surplus, wages for that labor will be reduced. The laws of supply and demand determine the relative wages among different types of labor.

But this still does not tell us what determines the wage level in an economy. There is a tendency for wages in an area to be linked together, so that one can speak of wages being generally high in Japan and low in India. Barbers in the United States have had a higher wage, even relative to local prices, than those in Mexico or Latvia, although their quality of work is similar.

George (pp. 26–7) recognized the "fundamental truth" that the basic principles of economics evident in a simpler, primitive, society are still in effect in a more complex, more developed world. We can discover the principles of wages by first analyzing a primal economy. Suppose there is a village that gets its food from hunting and gathering, and that there is more than enough land and game to support the village. The land is owned by the village in common, and since land is abundant, there it no rental value. Suppose also that the village is really primal, so that they don't have significant capital goods—no tools, like baskets or spears.

If the villagers go naked into the bush and gather nuts and berries with their bare hands, the only resources are land and labor. Here we see an economy in its most fundamental form:

a person "endeavoring to obtain from nature by the exertion of his powers the satisfaction of his desires" (George, p. 27). Since there is no rent, the fruit they gather is all wages. Leaving out capital goods for now, what the naked hunters get from the forest, catching animals with their hands, is also wages. It is clear here that the hourly wage of the hunter/gatherer is equal to the produce that one can obtain from an hour's labor. Also clear is the principle that production precedes consumption.

When a laborer receives his wages in money instead of goods, the principle is the same. A worker "really receives in return for the addition his labor has made to the general stock of wealth, a draft upon that general stock ..." (p. 29). Thus, money wages too are not economically an advance but only a claim on the amount of value one's labor has added to.

George notes, further, that all workers contribute to the production of all wealth. For example, the person who repairs fish nets helps catch the fish as much as the ones who go out into the sea. But the one who made the boat also contributed to the catch. And so did the one who made the wood and steel for the boat. Extending this to its logical conclusion, everyone who labors helped catch those fish. You as a worker help produce bread and steel by demanding these products in exchange for the goods you helped to make as well as by contributing ultimately to the goods that the bread maker and steel maker need. As George (p. 77) put it, "in aiding in the production of what other producers want, he is directing other labor to the production of the things he wants—in effect, producing them himself."

If we then add tools and buildings and other capital goods, labor is able to obtain more product, but again, the portion earned by labor in general will be its marginal (extra) contribution to the product. If land rent is zero, then since capital goods are produced by labor, both the tool maker and consumer-goods maker obtain their wages from their product. In practice, individual workers might get paid more or less than the economic value of their product due to personal biases of bosses, imperfect knowledge, inadequate or superior negotiating skills, or luck, but the general tendency in a pure market economy is for wages to equal the marginal product that labor provides.

Now, perhaps because the forest is destroyed, the society turns to farming. Each family gets a plot that it farms. Suppose it can grow 10 bushels of corn per unit of land per some period of time. They have as much land as they want of that quality, so rent is still zero. Again leaving capital goods aside, the 10 bushels grown by a farmer is all wages. Clearly, wages are drawn from the goods it produces, and in any particular area, the amount and value of the goods that labor can produce determines the wage.

The fact that some goods are produced over a long period of time does not change the principle. As George (pp. 50–51) notes, if a shoemaker starts with leather and works it up into a pair of shoes, the labor has gradually added more and more value to the original capital good, the leather. Hence the wage comes from the value added rather than from the original capital. As George (p. 56) put it, "Production is always the mother of wages."

B) The extensive margin

Suppose now that the most productive land, where farmers can grow 10 bushels, is all taken up. Farmers will now cultivate the next best area, which we can consider to be 9-bushel land. Wages at the 9-bushel land are 9. What, then are wages now in the 10-bushel land? If someone offers a wage of 9.5, all the farmers in the 9-bushel land will come running to apply. Someone who wants to hire labor only needs to pay 9 bushels. If he offers any less, no one applies, since they can get 9 by working for themselves.

If someone owns a farm on the 10-bushel land and hires a worker instead of working on it himself, that extra bushel produced after paying 9 to the employee is therefore not wages, but goes to the owner as rent.

So wages in all land are equalized, due to competition among the workers, and any extra product goes to the owners of the lands as rent.

The best available land that can be had for free is called the "extensive" margin of production. It is called "extensive" because people keep extending or moving it out to lands of ever lesser quality as the better land gets taken up. The wage level is determined at the extensive margin, where the best free land is available. This boundary is also called the margin of cultivation, or more generally, for lands of all uses, the margin of production.

It is only when the margin is pushed further and further away and people are located on worse and worse land that the base rate of wages will fall. As George (p. 206) stated, "the wages which an employer must pay will be measured by the lowest point of natural productiveness to which production extends, and wages will rise or fall as this point rises or falls." If people are pushed to production on the land on which one can barely survive, then wages will be at a subsistence level.

In Great Britain, at the time when people set off to colonize Australia, wages were low. With labor competing for limited opportunities and no free good land available, employers could afford to offer low wages. However, in Australia, New Zealand, and America, the situation was reversed. Land taken from the aboriginal inhabitants was available to European immigrants, and it had a much higher yield than the margin in Europe. Therefore, wages for other occupations had to be high to keep employees.

Suppose in some island all the land gets taken up. There is no more free land. The margin, however, is still there, if not for agriculture, then for something else. One can go to the sea and catch fish in waters where one does not have to pay rent. In towns, one can add an extra story or build a two-story instead of one-story building; the margin would then be vertical space, where the top stories of buildings are located, since another story can be built without paying any more for land. There is almost always some type of land, whether air, water, or surface soil, that is available.

If we now switch from a one-crop economy to many crops, different products, we see that labor can be used to produce one or the other. The value of the labor, its wages, will be determined by the values that the customers and consumers of the crops place on those products. If one person grows sour apples and few people want them, then his wage will be low. If there is a high demand for the good, the wage, over the time of production, will be high.

Workers will then tend to move from low-paid to higher-paid products, if they can. If workers are growing mangos and lemons, and one mango is trading for one papaya, but it takes twice as much work to grow the papaya as the mango, the mango growers will have a wage twice that of the papaya growers. If some workers are willing to switch from one crop to another, wages will tend to equalize among the crops or, more generally, among products, resulting in some overall wage level. More mangos will be produced and fewer papayas, reducing the relative price of mangos until one papaya trades for two mangos.

Hence, the principle remains the same in complex production, where we have many products and industries. The "law of wages," as Henry George (p. 213) called it, is that "Wages depend upon the margin of production." More generally, the wage level is determined by the margin of production, the least productive land in use, and the intensive margin where the next worker can get the highest wage without having to pay extra rent.

C) The marginal product of labor

What happens if one of the farm owners that has hired a worker wishes to hire a second worker? The second one is also paid the same wage as people can get by working on their own farms, but is the extra product of this worker the same? We now turn to the interaction between wages and the productivity of workers on the same lot of land, or in the same factory or enterprise.

The "marginal product of labor" is the increase in total output achieved by hiring one more laborer. If by raising the work force from 50 to 51 a firm raises total output from 1000 to 1010 units, then the marginal product of labor is 10. The "value of the marginal product" is the physical marginal product (the extra goods produced) times the price of the product.

Suppose we have a farm of 100 acres (40 hectares). One farmer by himself might be able to grow 100 bushels of corn during a certain time. If a second farmer is hired, the total product might grow to 240. The marginal product of the second farmer is 140, since the two can do some things that the first could not by himself. A third farmer might raise total product to 350. He adds 110 to product, less that the second, since there is less marginal benefit from the added cooperation and work. Although in any particular case, the first few added workers may each add more to output than the previous, eventually, the added or marginal product must decline, since the fixed factor, in this case land, will not yield increased output forever. This was the third foundational proposition of economics, as presented in Chapter 1.

The phenomenon of each new laborer (or other factor) adding ever less marginal product is called the "law of variable proportions," or, more famously, the "law of diminishing returns," also the "law of diminishing marginal product." Eventually, the diminishing marginal product becomes negative as workers keep getting added to a fixed amount of land.

The wage at the internal margin, or "intensive" margin (since a given lot of land or a factory gets used more and more intensively), must equal the wage at the extensive margin, due to competition among workers. It is possible that due to the high costs of labor or enterprise imposed by taxes and restrictive regulations, the cost of labor to an employer can be higher than the marginal product of labor, so that no more labor is hired, resulting in unemployment.

When the marginal product is greater than the average product, it pulls the average up, and when it is less, it pulls the average down. Therefore, the marginal product equals the average product when the average product is at its maximum. A rational producer, who wishes to have as high a profit as possible, will only hire workers when the marginal product is less than the average product but still positive.

Getting back to our earlier example, suppose that the margin of production is still at 10-bushel land, and one of the owners wants to hire a second worker. If the marginal product of the first worker is 10 but that of a second worker is only 9, the owner would not offer him more than 9 bushels as wages. But no one would want to be a second worker, since one could earn 10 as a first worker on his own land.

But suppose that the population grows and all the 10-bushel land is taken up. The extensive margin moves to the 9-bushel land. The owner will now be willing to hire an extra worker, and will be especially willing if the margin moves to just below 9, so he can pay a wage of less than 9 and get some extra rent. In general, an employer will hire more workers as long as their marginal product is greater than the wage. Since the marginal product eventually declines, workers are hired just up to the amount where the value of their marginal product, that extra revenue produced by that extra worker, just equals the wage.

Since a firm will hire labor at the amount that equals its value of marginal product, and since that marginal product declines with increasing numbers of workers, a firm's demand curve for labor is exactly the relation between its value of marginal product and the number of workers, whether depicted as a curve in a graph or a table of numbers. The firm's demand curve for labor will thus slope down, since it demands more workers as the wage declines.

It should be kept in mind that though conceptually the demand for labor seems to be a precise thing, in practice the marginal product is a fuzzy, uncertain, imprecise amount, so the demand curve or relationship for labor, like any demand or supply curve, is a fuzzy rather than sharply defined line or table. Also, as we know, other factors can affect the demand for a particular worker, such as his looks, personality, ethnic background, personal relationship with an employer, and just plain luck! So the equation of wage with marginal product is a general tendency rather than exact description for every worker.

What about the demand for labor by an entire economy? It is the result of the demand for labor by all firms, but this "demand" itself is derived from productivity, since self-employed workers are their own demanders. We can envision a "production function" for the entire economy, i.e. total output as a function of the number of workers.

Since labor exhibits diminishing returns relative to the land in any particular region or economy, total output goes up with increasing labor, but at a slowing rate of growth, each extra worker adding a bit less to output than the previous. That extra output is none other than the wage of the extra worker, so we have a downward-sloping demand for labor as a whole in an economy, wages declining with increasing labor at any particular moment. But it is important to note, and note well, that this is a static relationship between labor and output. It applies to the amount of labor at any particular moment in time, not to the addition of workers in an economy over time, which could also increase the division of labor and dynamically increase output per worker.

The supply of labor for an entire economy, or the market supply curve, is the quantity of the labor force (all workers plus the unemployed who want to work) as a function of the wage level. In other words, it is a curve showing the number of workers at each wage level. Its exact shape depends on the culture and demographics (of age, sex, family size) in a particular economy. It is possible in some places for the curve to bend backwards, or be upward-sloping at some wage level, because with higher wages, the workers will not want to work so many hours, preferring leisure to more consumer goods.

Generally, one would expect the curve to be rather flat at the subsistence level, since every family needs to eat, up to the number of families. Then it would slope up as second or third members of a family are willing to work at higher wages, and workers are more willing to work overtime or take less leisure. But then at a very high wage, the curve would become very steep, vertical, and then slope back as workers have a greater marginal desire for leisure time rather than more goods.

As with any market, the wage level would be determined at the intersection of the market supply and demand curves. With that type of market supply curve for labor, wages would be high if the demand curve crosses it at the steeply rising area. This would occur if the marginal product of labor is high to begin with, in which case the supply curve would become steep or vertical after all families have applied their labor. Increasing demand for labor, or productivity, would only raise the wage without increasing the labor supply much. But if the demand curve for labor hits the supply curve at the horizontal section, then an outward shift (increase) in demand would increase employment without increasing wages.

4. HOW TO CREATE UNEMPLOYMENT AND IMPOVERISH WORKERS

The above analysis assumes that there is no tax on wages. If wages are taxed, then the worker receives a lower net wage, so if the supply curve is sloping up, then there will be less labor supplied, since the worker responds to the take-home wage net of taxes. Thus, a tax on wages, such as a payroll or income tax, shifts the supply-of-labor curve to the left. As the supply curve shifts up along the demand curve, this increases the cost of labor to the employers. Employers must pay the gross wage, including the tax. The result is less employment at a higher cost to employers, and a lower net wage for workers. The tax is a "wedge" between the net and gross wage, which distorts or skews the market wage to employers and employees from what a pure market would yield.

To see the effect of taxes on labor, suppose there were a tax of $1 million per worker. Almost all workers would be thrown out of work, including the self-employed. The effect of a smaller tax is the same; the difference is only in degree. The higher the wage tax, the less employment.

Henry George (1883, p. 152) stated, "The essence of slavery is the robbery of labor." With chattel slavery, as existed in the 19th century and earlier, the slave owner expropriates the product of the slave's labor, beyond what the slave keeps to live on. "Free" labor has a choice of whom to work for, but if wages are taxed, labor is also deprived. It is not working for an employer puts a worker at a disadvantage, since in a free economy, he has the option of working for himself. Rather, it is being forced to work for others to the extent that part of one's wages is taken by government.

Another type of intervention in the labor market is minimum wages. If the minimum wage set by the government is higher than that of a market wage level, the quantity supplied of labor is increased, since more people want to work, while the quantity demanded is decreased, since labor is more expensive. The result is an excess or glut of workers wanting to work but not finding it: unemployment. Minimum wages especially affect teenagers and those wanting to enter the labor market, since they are unable to get entry-level work that would give them experience to enable them to get better jobs later.

Thus, if a government wants to reduce employment and keep workers unemployed, a good way to do this is to tax labor heavily and also enact a minimum wage, in addition to restricting entry into some types of occupations. This has been the policy of the U.S. and other governments, and it has been quite effective in keeping many workers poor and unemployed.

5. LABOR UNIONS

Low wages and bad working conditions are two reasons why labor unions have organized. Trade unions arose out of the conditions of the labor force during the Industrial Revolution. Workers could gain bargaining power through collective action, of which the most potent weapon is the strike. Unions also became mutual aid societies, offering various services to their members.

Unions can be effective in giving laborers more bargaining power in a particular industry, but they cannot increase the overall wage level, since, as discussed above, that level depends on the productivity of labor, which cannot be increased solely by a labor strike. If an economy is divided into two labor sections, one with unions and the other without, then where they have labor monopolies, unions raise the wages of workers in those industries, reducing employment there. The workers thrown out of work will then move to the non-union sector, increasing the labor supply and so decreasing the wage level there.

Thus the effect of unions is to transfer income from the non-union section to the union section. The pushed-up wages in unionized industries also increase the prices of those products, decreasing the quantity bought, so part of the cost of these union wages are borne by consumers.

This does not imply that labor unions are harmful in general, only that they reduce employment and output in an industry when they have a legally enforceable monopoly power. Labor unions can and have been useful in organizing social benefits for their members and in serving as a way to communicate in an organized way with the management of enterprises to negotiate better working conditions. But unions by themselves, whether voluntary or coercive, cannot raise the overall wage level or decrease unemployment. As analyzed above, the way to maximize wages and employment is to remove the barriers, wage controls, and tax costs imposed on labor.

6. RAISING WAGES THROUGH EDUCATION

As noted above, "human capital," education and training which increases the productivity of labor, is part of the labor factor. The general wage level is based on that of unskilled labor. Workers obtain a wage premium above the unskilled wage level for their skill, talent, charm, and personal connections, and the scarcity of workers in the field. There can also be premiums or discounts due to discrimination and legal restrictions.

An individual worker can make himself more marketable relative to others by increasing his skill, including his skill at job finding. But when most workers attain similar skills, the comparative advantage of the skill will be lost, although there will still be an absolute advantage in being better trained. As we know, for education to increase productivity, it needs to be geared either to general skills such as reading and writing, or to the specific requirements of a field. A general education is also useful over the long run both for personal consumption, to better enjoy life, and to be a good citizen.

Education presumes the freedom to make use of it. When opportunities are blocked off, education makes a person frustrated. In some less-developed countries, young people obtain a university education and then find no job opportunities, other than the civil service, which expands to give them jobs, but without any productive purpose. In a free society, employment opportunities are abundant, and education does not need to be highly subsidized, since most families can afford to pay tuition. Enterprises seeking skilled workers also offer training and scholarships. If government schooling is still provided, it is in equal competition with private schools, and this market competition maintains the quality of the education as well as providing different cultural settings. In a multi-cultural society, the problem of what to teach is resolved by the freedom to start new schools that offer education geared to the interests of the students and parents. Competitive schooling not only provides training and knowledge, but also preserves the cultural capital that is part of our diverse heritage.

Chapter 3: Land and its Rent

1. THE MEANING OF LAND

Economic land" consists of everything except human beings and the wealth that they have produced. We will call it "land" for short. Land of economic value consists of natural resources, including underground minerals, metals, and oil; wildlife, including forests; the genetic variety of life; oceans, lakes, and rivers; the atmosphere; the electro-magnetic spectrum (for transmitting radio and television); and the three-dimensional surface area of the earth as sites for living and working.

By definition, an item is economically scarce if there is not enough to provide as much as everyone wants at a zero price. As the first universal proposition of economic theory states, some land is scarce. Of these types of natural resources, the most familiar in every-day life is the surface area of the earth, the space that we live and work in. This land obtains a market value due to its usefulness over time and the scarcity of land of good qualities. This value is called "land rent."

2. RENT

The word "rent" has several meanings.

First, in everyday language the "rent" of an office, house, factory, or shop means a payment for the use of property, which includes the use of land as well as produced wealth, such as buildings, cars, and computers.

In classical economics, "rent" had a special meaning as the amount that one pays solely for the use of land. Thus, when we speak of the "rent of land" or the "rental value of land," in economics we exclude improvements such as buildings and canals.

The term "rent" later became generalized in two directions. First, "rent" came to mean any payment that is more than necessary to put some resource into production. This is called "economic rent." For example, if a baseball star would be earning $50,000 per year in his next best profession, but is earning $600,000 per year playing baseball, the $550,000 difference is called "economic rent" because the player would play ball for just a bit over $50,001.

This meaning of rent became used also to refer to the "economic rents" received by those seeking privileges and transfer payments from the government without really earning it; they are economic rent because the funds do not put any service into production. The attempt to get such loot is called "rent seeking" (better called "transfer seeking") in the literature dealing with this, a body of theory called "public choice."

We can see that land rent is a type of economic rent, since the land is there from nature, so no funds are needed to produce the land. To simplify the language, "rent" here will refer to economic land rent unless otherwise specified. The term "rental" will refer to the actual payments of tenants to landlords, which may differ from the economic rent of the land.

The word "rent" in economics differs from the ordinary usage in another way. In ordinary language, we say someone rents something only when a payment changes hands. You rent a house from someone when you pay the landlord a check every month. But in economics, "rent" exists regardless of whether there are explicit payments. For example, suppose your parents let you live for free in a house they own. If they didn't let you live there, they could "rent" it out for $500 per month. Suppose further more that $200 of this amount is due to the land value, while the other $300 is due to the improvements, such as the building. Then they are losing $200 per month from the land rent which they could have collected. This $200 is rent even though no payments change hands. In effect, you the resident are collecting it, since you would otherwise be paying it if someone else owned it. So the amount of rent that a landowner could get on the market is economic rent whether or not the owner collects it in payments. If you own and work your own farm, the amount that you could have rented the land for is economic rent.

The value of land can be expressed in one of two ways: (1) the amount of rent offered for a fixed term of use, e.g. a week, month, or year; or (2) the transfer price when one obtains title for either a "leasehold" (possession of land for a fixed term such as 99 years) or a "freehold" (indefinite possession). As stated by Henry George (1879, p. 166), "Rent is also expressed in a selling price. When land is purchased, the payment which is made for the ownership, or right to perpetual use, is rent commuted or capitalized. If I buy land for a small price and hold it until I can sell it for a large price, I have become rich, not by wages for my labor or by interest upon my capital, but by the increase in rent."

In the simplest case, with no taxes, no collection of the rent by a community beyond the title holder, no price appreciation, and no inflation, the sale price tends to equal to the rent divided by the interest rate: $p = r / i$. This is because $r = p * i$ (rent equals the principal or price of land times the interest rate), since the same funds (p) if loaned out at interest rate i would yield the annual amount r. If the money is inflating, then we need to subtract out inflation from the interest rates being paid in order to get the "real" interest rate I. If there is a tax on the land, or the collection of the land rent by a community, then the collection rate is added to the interest rate, since the rent must pay for both the tax and the net yield to the title holder: $r = p * (i + t)$, where t is the tax rate, the percentage of land value being collected, such as 5% of p. Therefore,

$p = r / (i + t)$. Hence, as i or t or both increase, the price of land decreases. If rent increases, then of course the price increases.

3. HOW DOES RENT ARISE?

The value of land is due to a variety of sources. We can divide land into three types: 1) fixed material resources, 2) renewable resources, and 3) space. Fixed material resources include minerals, oil, metals in the ground, and air. Renewable resources include wildlife, the fertility of the soil, sunlight, and fresh water. The value of material land is due to its scarcity relative to human desires for these items. Oil and minerals are land as long as they are in their natural state; once people apply effort to extracting them or even exploring for them, then the value added is a capital good.

Some space on earth is not scarce, since one may go to the oceans or deserts and freely use all the space one desires. Space obtains value because for a particular use, in a given location, it is scarce; more space for that use cannot be obtained for free. For space, as recognized by Henry George (p. 166), "rent or land value does not arise from the productiveness or utility of land … but upon its capacity as compared with that of land that can be had for nothing."

4. THE DETERMINATION OF RENT

Suppose a new island arose in the middle of the Atlantic Ocean. It has many thousands of hectares and acres of fertile land. An international agreement allows anyone to settle on the land and claim plots of 100 acres or 40 hectares. To keep our model from being needlessly complicated, there will be only one crop: corn. The unit of output is bushels per acre per time unit. We will fix the time unit so that the best land grows 10 bushels in that amount of time. Also, to simplify at first, we will ignore capital goods and merge them with labor. Later, we will separate out capital goods. For now, there is only the original factors of production, land, and labor.

The foundational principles which were set forth in Chapter 1 can now be applied. Principle #2 states that resources vary in quality. We will let the land be divided into areas which grow 9, 8, 7, 6, 5, 4, 3, 2, 1, and zero bushels, depending on the sunlight, rain, soil, and elevation of various areas.

Now the first family arrives. In our model, there is only one farm worker per family, and all workers have the same ability and put forth the same work effort. Where, then, will the first family settle? Principle #12 states that people economize; they seek to produce a given amount with the least effort, or produce as much as possible with a given amount of effort. With land of different quality, the most will be produced with a given amount of effort on the best, most productive land. Naturally, the first family will settle on the 10-bushel land. Other settlers will also settle on that best land.

Since the best land is available for free, no one can charge a rent for the land that he possesses. So rent is zero. And since we are ignoring capital, all the production goes to wages. Since production on the best land is 10, wages are equal to 10.

Once the 10-bushel land has been settled, newcomers will go to the next best land, where they can grow 9 bushels. Wages on that land are therefore 9. But what about wages in the 10 land?

Suppose one of the owners of a 10-farm wishes to retire, and hires someone to work the farm. He offers a wage of 8. No one from the 9 land will take up the offer, since they can get 9 working on their own farms. If he were to offer 9.5, everyone from the 9 land would want to get hired since that is more than what they can get on their own farms. So competition will set the wage offered at just 9, where someone is indifferent between working in the 10 or the 9 land. Wages everywhere are 9. Note that, as discussed in Chapter 2, this is the principle of how wages are determined: they are set where the best land is available without rent, since any wage offer below this will not be accepted and any above this will have many competitive takers who will drive down the wage.

But what about that extra bushel on the 10 land after the wage of 9 has been paid? Since this is not wages, it must be a return to the other factor, land. The 1 bushel left over is rent. The 10 land has acquired a rent of 1 when cultivation moved to the 9 land.

As discussed in Chapter 2, the boundary where people are settling on the best free land is called the "margin of cultivation." More generally, for land of all uses, the boundary is called the "margin of production." The term "margin" means the edge of consumption or production, where the last unit of a resource or the last item of consumption is being used. The margin of cultivation is the very next acre or hectare of land that would be occupied for farming.

Suppose now that after that one farmer hired on the 10 land, the owner decides to hire a second farmer on the same land, since that would increase output even more. He pays the second one 9 bushels and sees that the yield is now 18.5. The second farmer only added 8.5 bushels to output. The marginal product of labor is 8.5, while the wage is 9, so the second worker is dismissed. As noted in Chapter 2, labor will only be hired in a competitive economy if the marginal product is higher or at least equal to the prevailing wage.

When all the 9-bushel land is taken, the margin of cultivation moves to the 8-bushel land. Wages are now 8. Hence, rent on the 9-bushel land is now 1, and rent on the 10-bushel land has gone up to 2. Now that wages have been reduced to 8, the owner of that 10-bushel farm can hire that extra worker. The marginal product is 8.5, leaving the owner 1.5 bushels as rent. So all the owners of the 10-bushel land hire two workers (those working their own farms hire themselves and another), increasing their rent to 2.5. Land in the 10-bushel area rents for 2.5, since that is what can be obtained by hiring the optimal number of workers for the maximum possible rent. The population density on the 10 land will now be twice that of the other lands.

We can now derive the determination of rent in general. Rent in a certain location is the highest product of land above what can be produced at the margin of production, where rent is zero, after paying for the factors of production other than land. This is called "differential rent" because the rent at a location arises from the differential or extra product it yields (minus costs for labor and capital goods) compared to land at the margin. All land rent is thus differential rent.

This differential rent is also the marginal product of land, the extra amount of product obtained from using an extra amount of land, keeping other factors constant. Hence if with two workers one gets a tiny additional amount of 10 land, it too will yield a proportional equivalent of 2.5 (18.5 minus wages of 16) per acre too, and the marginal product after subtracting wages will be 2.5 per acre. So the marginal product of land is the same as the differential rent.

More settlers arrive; the 8-bushel land gets filled, and the 7-bushel land is settled. Wages fall to 7. Rent on the 8 land is now 1. Rent on the 9 land rises to 2. But those owners too now hire a second worker, since the product of the second worker on the 9 land is 7.5, which increases the total product to 16.5, which after paying 14 for wages, leaves 2.5 in rent.

In the 10 land, a third worker will have a marginal product of 7 and rent is now 4.5 (3 from the product of the first, plus 1.5 from the product of the second worker). Owners will be indifferent to hiring a third worker; some may and some may not, depending on whim or chance.

When the margin of cultivation moves to 6, the 7-bushel land gets a rent of 1 and the 8-bushel land rent rises to 2 if there is one worker. Keeping the marginal product of the second worker at 1.5 less than the first, second workers are hired on the 8-bushel land, since their marginal product is 6.5, raising the total rent there to 2.5.

Rent on the 9-bushel land rises by one bushel to 3.5 (a third worker's product is 6, just equal to the wage). In the 10 land, total product with three workers is 10 + 8.5 + 7, totaling 25.5, with wages 3*6=18, leaving 7.5 for rent.

Can you see the pattern that develops? As the margin of cultivation moves to ever less productive land, wages go down and rent goes up. The owners of the best land obtain higher and higher incomes due to the increase in population and the decrease in the marginal productivity of land. Incomes thus become more and more unequal. As settlement proceeds further, wages will be driven down to the subsistence level, where workers are just able to survive—a level in fact being earned by many of the poor around the world, including in developed countries.

5. LAND SPECULATION

In the above model, we assume that each farmer gets a lot for actual use. But there is another motive for getting land. Folks will notice that the rent is going up and up on the older lands as the margin moves to newer land that is less productive. So some sharpies will obtain land not just for use but to get the increase in the rent in the future.

Suppose, for example, that the 8-bushel land is being settled. The speculators will try to claim as much of the 8 land as possible, since it is free now but will have a rent when the margin moves to 7. So those wanting some 8 land for farming will find that the 8 land will be all claimed very quickly. When production moves to the 7 land, farmers can either rent land in the 8 region or claim 7 land. They will prefer to claim 7 land in the hopes of getting rent when the margin moves to 6, so much of the 8 land will remain vacant for a while. Eventually, the sites in 8 land get rented, but there is now a rush to occupy 7 land, and then 6 land, and so on, leaving much of it vacant as the margin quickly moves to ever less productive land.

So the effect of excessive land speculation is to move the margin out much more rapidly, reducing wages and increasing rents that much sooner. Excessive land speculation also increases the price of land for current use, since the price reflects the expected future usage. Land speculation is excessive when the land value is subsidized by government, as the infrastructure and services of government raise rents, while financed by taxes on labor and capital rather than having landowners pay back the generated rent.

6. THE EFFECT OF CAPITAL GOODS

Capital goods will be examined in the next chapter, but let's fill out our model briefly by including them now. Let's start again in the 10-bushel land.

Suppose that farmers were somehow growing the corn with their bare hands, but then someone invents some tools that enable them to double production. These tools, however, only last one month. If half the farmers spend a month making the tools instead of farming, the farmers as a whole are no better off, since only half the workers are now farming, so at twice the crop per worker, the total yield is the same. Hence, the resources needed to make the tools must more than offset the greater productivity from the tools.

Suppose instead that the tools double the monthly output per farmer and last three months. A farmer could make tools one month and use them for three months. The total product would be 60 for the four months, for a monthly average of 15. So the marginal product of the tools, the capital goods, would be 5 per month. Some of the workers might become full-time tool makers. They would trade their tools for 15 bushels of corn every month. They therefore earn a wage of 15, and the farmers also earn 15 per month, after growing 20 bushels and paying 5 to the tool maker every month (for a total of 15 for three months).

We can see that the capital goods have increased productivity by 10, but only 5 is paid to the tool maker, so wages have increased by 50%. The increase in productivity is split between wages and the yield from making capital goods. (We ignore interest rates, which would only slightly affect the calculations). This is because, at the margin (where some workers are indifferent between farming and tool making), wages are equalized, so the return to making capital goods will tend to equal that of farming, assuming the quality of labor is the same.

With the tools doubling productivity in lands of all qualities, we can see that adding capital goods complicates the model but does not alter its essential principles. After the 10-bushel (now 20 bushel) land is used up, the margin will still move to the 9-bushel land (now doubled to 18). The now 20-bushel land will then acquire a rent, while wages will drop in the 18-bushel land as well as in the 20-bushel land from 15 to 13.5 (9 plus 4.5). Even if we suppose that tool makers do not pay rent (living with farmers, for example), the rent on the 20 bushel land is now 2, having doubled while wages have only increased by 50% (since the other 50% is paid to the tool maker). So the effect of the capital goods in this example is to increase rent in proportion to the increased productivity, while only increasing wages by half the increased productivity. In general, the proportional increase in rent will tend to be higher than that of wages.

Wages will be higher because of the capital goods, but still diminish, along with the yield from making capital goods, as the margin is moved to less productive land. And if the capital goods enable one to use land that previously was unproductive, the margin might be extended to the level where wages are no higher than they were without the capital goods.

So the accumulation of capital goods and technical progress, including a more efficient division of labor, can increase wages, offsetting the effect of the diminishing marginal product of labor, but if the margin of productivity then moves again to less productive land, the benefit of this increased product will again end up going to rent rather than wages or the owners of capital. In studying wages during the first decade of the 2000s, some economists concluded that average wages have remained about the same, while per-capita output rise. One explanation could be that the increase went to higher rent, and indeed, until the real estate boom crashed in 2008, land values were rapidly escalating.

7. URBAN RENT

The Austrian economist Friedrich von Wieser (1927 [1967], p. 340), an early theorist of urban rent, stated that "Urban rent is that part of the rental which is paid as a premium for the advantages of the better location." Urban rent arises with the presence of a population and its economic activities.

That people and their collective activities give rise to rent can be seen by looking at any densely populated city. Equally, one can look at those places that have "gone back" to their uninhabited or primitive state. Ghost towns in the American West, for example, which have collapsed through lack of industry or have been over-exploited, "mined out". When the town prospered, land titles had a rental value. Now, with the disappearance of the population, these land titles have become valueless. Rental value of land will clearly arise and collapse with that of populations and their activity.

Henry George (1879) theorized that the greatest effect on rent was the presence of communities rather than the extension of the margin of production to inferior land. He illustrated this effect with a story about the "unbounded savannah," a field "stretching off in unbroken sameness of grass and flower …" (p. 235). Along comes a first immigrant family. Nature is rich with resources, but this single family has to provide for all its needs, so though they have enough to eat, they have little wealth.

Another family comes along, and though the land is the same everywhere, "there is one place that is clearly better for him than any other place, and that is where there is already a settler and he may have a neighbor" (p. 236). The two families may now cooperate to produce wealth previously too difficult for one. (Although if the first family likes solitude or has a lifestyle (such as nudism or loud music) that the second does not like, then the second one might settle just far enough away for privacy but close enough for cooperation when needed.)

As more settlers arrive, they tend to locate near each other. They may form several communities with different values and lifestyles, but there will tend to be one major settlement where many services have become available, and those smaller outer communities also join in to form one greater community. "Labor has now an effectiveness which, in the solitary state, it could not approach" (p. 237). They can cooperate to accomplish large tasks, and can also create a division of labor for specialized work such as teaching. "Satisfactions become possible that in the solitary state were impossible."

Now, says George, go to our first settler and offer him the full value of all his improvements. "He would laugh at you. His land yields no more wheat or potatoes than before, but it does yield far more of all the necessaries and comforts of life … The presence of other settlers—the increase of population—has added to the productiveness, in these things, of labor bestowed upon it, and this added productiveness gives it a superiority over land of equal natural quality where there are as yet no settlers" (pp. 238–9).

Let the population continue increasing, and now the town has grown into a great city. The "division of labor becomes extremely minute, wonderfully multiplying efficiency ... Hither run all roads, hither set all currents, through all the vast regions round about. Here, if you have anything to sell, is the market; here, if you have anything to buy, is the largest and choices stock" (p. 240). Here are the great libraries, specialists, and center of commerce and government.

"So enormous are the advantages which this land now offers for the application of labor, that instead of one man with a span of horses scratching over acres, you may count in places thousands of workers to the acre, working tier upon tier ... All these advantages attach to the land, ... for here is the center of population—the focus of exchanges, the market place and workshop of the highest forms of industry. The productive powers which density of population has attached to this land are equivalent to the multiplication of its original fertility by the hundredfold and the thousandfold. And rent, which measures the difference between this added productivity and that of the least productive land in use, has increased accordingly" (p. 241).

The increasing rent that is generated by an increasing population and the growth of communities thus comes about "not so much from the necessities of increased population compelling the resort to inferior land, as from the increased productiveness which increased population gives to the lands already in use" (p. 242).

8. RENT AS SURPLUS, AND WHY LAND IS DIFFERENT FROM LABOR

Sir William Petty (1623–1687), an English economist, was among the first in Europe to examine the nature of rent. Petty regarded the rent of land as a surplus arising after the labor costs of production have been met.

Adam Smith (1723–1790) presented the theory in similar terms. Rent, according to Smith, was a surplus which arose after the basic costs of production had been met. Thus, improvements in the efficiency of production, which reduced costs, raised the surplus income, and subsequently translated into higher rent: "All those improvements in the productive powers of labour, which tend to directly reduce the real price of manufactures, tend indirectly to raise the real rent of land ... Every increase in the real wealth of society, every increase in the quality of useful labour employed within it, tends indirectly to raise the real rent of land" (1776 [Book I, Chapter XI, Conclusions], pp. 275–6).

A more complete explanation of how rent is measured was developed by David Ricardo (1772–1823). In 1817, he published the *Principles of Political Economy and Taxation*, in which he developed what has since been termed "The Law of Rent." The law states: the rent of land is determined by the excess of its produce over that which the same application of labor and capital goods can secure from the least productive land in use. As we have seen above, this law needs to be qualified to take into account the intensive margin of land, where one lot is being worked with more and more labor. Because more labor is used by the more productive land, lands do not all have the same application of labor and capital goods; land rent will be even higher in the more productive land due to its greater intensity of use, as we have seen in the above model.

9. GENERALIZATION TO ALL LAND

The agricultural model used above can be generalized to land for all uses. For example, a grocery store in a sparsely settled area will have much less sales volume than one in the center of a large town. One would then expect much of this volume to be distributed to the owner of the site as rent, and indeed, rent in urban centers is much higher than in the rural boondocks. Offices in the center of metropolitan areas pay much higher rent than those in smaller towns. Generally, productivity of any sort generates higher rents relative to lower productivity. The law of rent applies to all land.

An important aspect of productivity is the availability of transportation, both of roads and of vehicles such as trains. This can best be understood by reference to a historical example. During the colonization of Australia and New Zealand, the first settlers to arrive naturally took up the most desirable sites. These sites were nonetheless looked upon by the British Colonial Office as marginal land which commanded little rent. The land was therefore sold for a low price. As further settlers arrived, they occupied less desirable sites. Eventually, the originally occupied sites, which previously had no value, were now prime sites in the center of towns and cities.

Those late arrivals settling on the new margin—remote sites far away from the center of town—faced increasing costs for transport to bring their produce to town. To have occupied sites closer to their markets, they would have had to bid a higher rent. The sites closer to town have lower transport costs and therefore higher profits per bushel of output, hence are more productive in terms of revenues minus all costs. This extra productivity induces the higher rent closer to town.

The theorist who developed the economics of location, including transportation, was Johann Heinrich von Thünen (1783–1850). In his work *The Isolated State* (1826), he explained that there was a relationship between transportation costs and the rental value of land. A farmer working on the periphery of a market area has the furthest to travel, therefore his land would have a low or zero rent. But suppose the roads leading to this marginal land were improved by the government. The reduction in transport costs results in a higher income per bushel of crop. (Similarly, improvements such as refrigeration further reduce the cost of transporting produce.) As we have seen in the above model, such increases in productivity increases the rent for the land affected. So much of the productivity due to the physical infrastructure—roads, trains, busses, communications—ends up as increased land rent.

Typically, financial firms, such as banks, have sought to locate in the center of town. A close proximity to commerce, government, and customers was needed before the advent of telecommunications. Despite modern communications for both voice and data, including money, financial firms still seek to locate themselves within the center, and rents in financial centers are among the highest. This is because of the extremely high rewards which banks, insurance headquarters, brokerage firms, etc., stand to gain through their location on these sites as opposed to locating on marginal sites.

The same principle applies to the location of commercial office blocks within a city. A firm will wish to locate its offices on a site which has easy access to the services on which it depends, such as transportation (subways, busses) for its customers and workers, and it might also need access to centrally located financial or governmental agencies. There will be a location beyond which the office cannot afford to locate itself—where the costs of getting its staff to work and of not being closer to complementary services becomes too high. Turning now to industrial activities, these too will have a margin beyond which it is unprofitable for them to locate. Some industries will be attracted to "economies (advantages) of density" as well as by transportation, such as access to a major highway. Thus, the rent of this land too is determined by the increased rewards which the industry stands to gain through its location.

Housing also has a margin. If a family chooses to locate in the countryside, beyond the denser residential developments, it might find that communing costs (including time), longer access to facilities and lack of public amenities make its location economically unattractive. Rent is therefore lower, other things being equal, at the edge of town than nearer to the center, although of course negative factors such as crime and noise and crowding will decrease the desirability and thus the rent in parts of town that are run down, even if near the center. With cars and long-distance communing trains and busses, people can live far from city centers, but still, one would not normally live hundreds of miles and kilometers from a city center; there is some limit to commuting times. And rent in the more desirable neighborhoods near the center of a city will fetch that much more rent than sites yonder.

Hence, each activity has some margin beyond which it will be unprofitable to locate. Generally, a city's economic activity takes place within the margins of the various functions. The corresponding rents are based on the rewards of location for an activity.

Much of land rent is generated by infrastructure and civic services. If landowners do not return the rent to pay for these goods, then they receive an implicit subsidy, and tenant-workers get double billed, having to pay both taxes and higher rent for these public goods.

10. THE SUPPLY AND DEMAND FOR LAND AND RENT

The quantity of fixed natural resources diminishes with increasing extraction, though the supply of known reserves of the resource increases when new sources are discovered. The supply of renewable resources is variable, making conservation and renewal essential if the supply is not to become extinct.

The surface space of the earth, however, is constant. Land area within any boundary is fixed in two ways: no space can be imported, and new space cannot be manufactured. Hence, for any particular region (given some boundary line), the amount of space is fixed. In a graph where the quantity of land is measured along the horizontal axis and the rent of land is on the vertical axis, the quantity of land is a vertical line at the amount (acreage, area) determined by the boundary. The supply of land for a particular use, or the supply of lots offered for sale, can vary with price and be upward sloping, but the quantity of surface sites within some area cannot be expanded or contracted.

The demand curve for a particular plot of land is the amount wanted at various prices. The demand curve slopes downwards, as greater amounts of land, like any product, are wanted at lower prices. So the diagonally downward-sloping demand curve cuts through the vertical supply curve at some point, determining the price of land. At the point where the curves intersect, of course, this demand is equal to the marginal product of land, the rent determined by its differential with respect to free land, or its capitalized value as the price of land.

If the demand for land in that area increases (more is wanted at each price), then the price of land will rise. But the supply will not be affected, since it is fixed. Also, if all or part of the rent is collected by a community, the supply of land will still not be affected. If the tax is higher than the rent, then people will no longer want to own land, and the tax will decrease the value of the capital goods tied to the land. So long as the amount of rent collected is not greater than the rent, it has no effect on the demand for the land and thus neither reduces nor increases the rental paid by the tenant. If the landlord is already charging as much rent as possible, the entire collected rent is borne by the landlord, and none of it can be passed onto the tenant.

However, the burden of a tax on land value is only borne by the owner at the time the tax rate is increased. Because the price of land falls, a new owner basically has no burden, because the tax payment replaces what would have been paid as mortgage interest (or the implicit return on his down payment). Since land rent is a pure surplus, after the transition, a tax on the rent or land value is not a burden even to the landowner.

11. MONOPOLY POWER IN LAND

At a speech given in Edinburgh, Scotland, in July, 1909, Winston Churchill observed "it is quite true that the land monopoly is not the only monopoly which exists, but it is by far the greatest of monopolies—it is a perpetual monopoly, and it is the mother of all other forms of monopoly" (Churchill, 1909, p. 149).

An "absolute monopoly" means an industry with one seller. But the term "monopoly" has a broader meaning. An "entry" monopoly exists when it is impossible to expand the supply of a good; a new firm can only buy title of an existing supply from the previous title holder.

Since land in a specific location is unique, each plot has a locational micro-monopoly. But there is another sense of the term "monopoly" having to do with entry and exit into an industry. In a competitive industry, firms can enter not just to increase the number of firms but to increase the production of the output. Moreover, the product can also be imported when profits are above normal. Increased supplies reduce the profits in the industry to normal returns. But when the stock of the product is fixed, when the expansion of output is impossible, then this competitive condition does not exist, and in that sense, there is a monopoly of the product among those firms who share in the fixed stock (Foldvary, 1993). The economic rent can persist indefinitely.

The nature of land as a monopoly is furthered by the fact that it keeps indefinitely. Land as a locational site doesn't spoil or rot. When an area is developing and the price of land is rising, the title holder profits simply by owning the site even if it is not rented out. It may be more profitable to avoid building at present and wait until the other sites are developed, when the real estate can then be sold at higher price. Keeping land out of use or in inefficient current use (such as parking lots in a city center) is detrimental to current production. It is not a pure market phenomenon, but a subsidy to the landowner from receiving rent generated by the community. and the absence of the collection of that land rent by the community.

12. URBAN SPRAWL

Urban sprawl is the difference between the use of urban land and the amount that would be used, for the same output, in a pure free market. It is an excessive urbanization of the countryside surrounding a city relative to that which would occur in a pure market economy. A pure market economy, with land rents collected for public revenue, and no zoning laws restricting the efficient use of land, would result in compact cities where density gradually decreased to the edges instead of helter-skelter hodge-podge developments.

Sprawl damages the surrounding agricultural and natural land, decreases the efficiency of cities and leads to a considerable waste of infrastructure such as streets, highways, pipes, and lights. Much of the inefficiency consists of longer commuting times, more costlier transportation for agricultural and urban goods, and wasted fuel. Though the loss of good crop land through urban sprawl is a needless waste, the damage goes further. It induces farmers to move further afield, destroying wildlife habitats.

Zoning laws often mandate maximum densities, requiring plots to have minimum sizes. Changes in zoning have been required in planned communities in which homes are clustered together, leaving more room for shared open space (Foldvary, 1994). City laws also often restrict the number of people able to live in a residence if they are not related by family, and restrict the ability to rent out rooms. Laws also prohibit enterprise at home as well as mixed use of land.

Also contributing to urban sprawl is the subsidy of the public works serving the outer edges. The streets, freeways, water and sewer pipes, lighting, security, fire service, parks, schools, and other goods and services are provided at the expense of the taxpayers of the entire city or county, often with the aid of higher levels of governments, so that these are subsidies which the users of suburban land consider free. Not having to pay its cost increases the usage and demand for these goods.

Taxation is a major contributor to urban sprawl. Vertical use of space is penalized by the taxation of buildings, while the horizontal use of space is subsidized. The remedy is the elimination of property taxes on improvements such as buildings and the funding of civic services from rent. In most cities, the high value land in the center is used inefficiently due to the secondary use of land as speculation. Land owners of central sites often have no incentive to redevelop their old buildings and can even leave central sites vacant. New development is displaced outward.

13. FARM SUBSIDIES

David Ricardo showed that if the state artificially raises the value of a product, such as corn, the value of the land that produces the good will rise. Ricardo wrote about the Corn Laws passed in England in the first decade of the 19th century. He showed that if you tax imported wheat (i.e. "corn") to raise its price to protect the British farmer, the rent of the corn land will go up. Rent will continue to rise until it has effectively wiped out the benefits to the farmer renting that land.

The *Lloyds Bank Economic Bulletin* (1992) reported that of the money spent under the European Economic Community's common agricultural policy, "around half is transferred to the land-owners and the rest is lost in inefficiency. Poor farmers and farm laborers appear to gain little." In Great Britain, it was calculated (Body, p. 209) that the total spent on agricultural subsidies since WWII is equal to the value by which farm lands have risen!

14. APPLICATION FOR PUBLIC REVENUE

As the factor of production that does not involve human exertion, and due to the fact that land is in fixed supply, land is the efficient and equitable source of revenue for governance and public goods. Chapter 16 on public finance discusses public revenue from land rent. Having analyzed the two factors labor and land, the next chapter discusses the third factor, capital goods.

Chapter 4: Capital Goods

1. DEFINITION

In Chapter 1, capital goods are defined as goods which have been produced but not yet consumed. Consumption means the using up of economic value, the way fire consumes wood. Production is the creation of economic value. If economic value is still there, such as for a car that still runs and has resale value, then the item remains a capital good.

An "economic investment" is an increase in the stock of capital goods and human capital (education and training). Thus, all production is economic investment. But the term "economic investment" is usually applied to the production of capital goods used by producers.

The economic consumption of a car is its depreciation, not its purchase. Capital goods tend to depreciate, to have their value used up, for two reasons. One is the tendency of most capital goods to wear down unless constantly maintained. The maintenance or repair is a production of new capital goods attached to the old one. The second cause of depreciation is obsolescence, as with an old computer that still runs, but has been superceded by bigger and faster machines.

The economist Nassau Senior is credited with forming "the abstinence theory of capital accumulation" (McConnel, 1980, p. 67). The theory states that land and labor are the primary factors in production; they are used to produce the third factor, capital goods. In order to provide tools, as illustrated by the model in Chapter 3, it is necessary to abstain from the production of immediate consumer goods in order to make the tools instead. Capital goods are produced to be used at a later stage in the production of more wealth.

Capital goods are more than inert matter. Embedded in them is technology that multiplies the productivity of land and labor, like a lever that enables one to lift a much heavier object. Capital goods also enable us to increase our division of labor, specializing in more fields and increasing the productivity in each field. For example, computer programmers and users can specialize in particular types and applications of software, and artists can specialize in particular types of media.

2. THE YIELD OF CAPITAL GOODS

Just as labor has a return as wages, and land as rent, capital goods have a return, which we can simply call a capital yield, with the understanding that this "capital" is capital goods. Economists once called this yield "interest," but this confusing usage is now obsolete, since interest earned from financial capital is not necessarily a return on capital goods.

The return on a capital good has two components. The first is that due to labor. The depreciation of capital goods include the using up of the labor value in the capital good and the using up of the value of the natural materials that went into the capital good. If you buy a tool that gets used up—depreciates—in one day and also takes one day to produce, the seller's return is, to him, a day's wage for his effort, which is also equal to the using up of the tool that day, in addition to the raw materials. Each day, he will make another tool that gets used up in one day. Wages will equal the labor portion of the depreciation.

But suppose, on the other extreme, that the tool lasts forever. The maker does not sell it, but loans it out. Since the tool does not depreciate, there is no labor component to the return of the owner. The labor portion was paid when the owner bought the tool. The tool never loses its value, so the labor component is retained as perpetual sales value, which the maker can obtain by its sale. The annual return on the tool is then the second component of a capital yield, the implicit interest. One could sell the tool and buy bonds that pay interest, and so there is an opportunity cost in owning the tool, the foregone interest, and thus the tool yields implicit interest.

Most capital goods neither depreciate immediately, nor last forever, so they will have a capital yield composed partly from depreciation and partly from implicit interest.

The fact that capital goods depreciate implies that a user of these goods needs to maintain or replace them. This capital maintenance is a cost of production even though it is not explicitly paid during some time interval; an accountant will enter an amount for depreciation as a cost. Hence, to calculate the economic profits or net income from an enterprise, depreciation needs to be subtracted from the gross income.

3. ROUNDABOUT PRODUCTION

Productivity can be increased if some production is devoted to indirectly producing a product, such as making the tools that the firm then uses to produce the final product, the crop. This is called "roundaboutness" or "roundabout production." Production becomes even more roundabout if some production is devoted, say, to making the steel and wood that is then used to make the tools for use in farming. As production becomes more roundabout, it takes longer from making the highest level capital good to its final use in the production of consumer goods. This increase in roundaboutness thus lengthens the period of production, the cycle of time needed to make the final good. This concept of greater productivity from greater roundaboutness of capital goods was developed by economists of the Austrian school of thought, especially by Eugen von Böhm-Bawerk.

The founder of the Austrian school, Carl Menger, originated Austrian capital-goods theory with the concept of "goods of higher order." Goods of lowest order are those with a quick turnover. Goods with a longer time of turnover are higher-order goods. Goods of the highest order require many years to mature into profit; the main higher-order capital good is real estate construction.

Menger also recognized that the time structure of capital goods has a relationship to the interest rate. Think of capital goods as a stack of pancakes, the bottom stack being circulating capital such as inventory that lasts only a few days, and the highest stack being real estate construction. When interest rates are lower, then it is more profitable to invest in goods of higher order, and when interest rates are relatively high, the rate of return is quicker and the structure of production flattens.

Suppose a tree takes 50 years to mature, and grows at at 3% per year. If the interest rate is 4%, the tree will not be planted. If the interest rate falls to 2%, then the tree is worth planting. When people save more, the interest rate falls, and there is more investment in higher-order goods, and that is offset by less consumption (since there is more savings), so all is in balance. Thus the interest is an equilibrium variable that adjusts to equalize savings and borrowing, and thus also savings and investment.

The structure of production, as affected by interest rates, has implications for business cycles, as worked out by F. A. Hayek, another Austrian economist. If money is injected into an economy by monetary policy, artificially reducing the interest rate, the capital structure will deepen as higher-order investment is stimulated. But since intended savings have not changed, consumers have not really reduced their demand for consumer goods, so this extra investment is not economically warranted. The result is inflation and a distortion of relative prices. When interest rates return to their previous level, the effect of the extra money having been dissipated by rising prices, the structure of capital flattens again, and investment in higher-order capital goods, such as buildings, slows and stops, as the recently produced goods become "malinvestments," wasted capital goods.

We saw this happen during the recession that began in December 2007. There was a large inventory of unsold and abandoned houses. Construction stopped, workers in real estate lost their jobs, and the fall in investment brought down the economy. (Business cycles will be covered depth in Chapter 12.)

If the use of capital goods achieves higher levels of return, we must have a means of measuring the increased yield. This takes the form of a rate of return or yield, also called "net productivity," which can be expressed in the form of a percentage per annum. To determine the rate of return of a capital project, first we calculate the costs of the factors we employ to undertake our capital project; then we calculate the total returns we stand to gain from the capital project, using the present value of the future gains. The excess of returns over costs will be our net productivity, and its ratio to costs the rate of return. Only if the total returns add up to more than the original costs do we have a positive net productivity, and only if the rate of return is greater than the prevailing interest rate (the alternative use of the funds) is it worth undertaking the capital project.

The rate of return on an investment in capital goods depends not only on the technical productivity of the roundabout process but on the market structure. For example, if a new process is protected by a patent, there will be less competition, and so the firm may charge a higher price for the output and get a greater return on the capital good. An entrepreneur creating capital goods needs to determine how much to invest in order to maximize his future return. We have already done some marginal analysis in previous chapters, so we need only apply the same principle regarding costs and benefits. A profit-maximizing firm will increase production up to the point at which marginal revenue equals marginal cost. If the marginal costs are increasing and the marginal revenues are decreasing, any more output and the firm would not be recovering its costs, and any less would result in the firm would not generating possible profits by expanding output.

4. RENTAL RETURNS TO CAPITAL GOODS

Some types of capital goods, such as infrastructure (streets, parks, transit, utilities) yield returns which manifest themselves in higher rentals and site values. An example would be a dam that prevents flooding and greatly reduces insurance costs. The civic goods provided by private communities, such as residential associations, shopping centers, and large resorts often raise both the land value within the community and that in the neighborhood. Since the improvements are capital goods rather than natural resources, this increase in the value of the sites is not land rent, but a capital yield, which takes the form of a rental on land as well as for the buildings. If the improvements were provided by private enterprise, then the generated rentals would be paid to those firms, by contract. If these capital goods are provided by government, then a tax on the value of the sites is partly a payment to government as provider of the civic goods.

As another example, the provision of water systems benefits the affected land-owners. This effect was documented in detail by L. R. East (former Chairman of the State Rivers and Water Supply Commission, Victoria, Australia). He wrote: "the real profits resulting from irrigation development lie not in the sale of water, but in the increases in business activities and in land values resulting from that development." East sites the "spectacular development" of the town of Sheparton, lying within one of the irrigation districts, as evidence that "there are very real benefits received by other sections of the community." Irrigation in Sheparton ultimately increased the value of land to 100 pounds a foot (1940's value) on its main business street (East, 1945, p. 7). A similar story to that of water supply could be told for the supply of railways, roads, and bridges. The process by which land-owners benefit is as follows: "the carrying out of public works such as roads, railways, and water supply makes possible increased production from the land, or more intensive use of the land, and as practically the whole advantage goes to the owner—as distinct from the worker engaged in production—this advantage is capitalised in increased land values" (p. 27). Some countries have had the vision to tap this rental capital yield in financing capital investments. Public works are thus funded by the subsequent increase in rent and land values. The huge Aswan Dam, which supplies Egypt's Nile Valley, was financed by an increase of 0.5 pounds an acre in the land tax over a very large area which received summer irrigations from the reservoir (p. 24).

The idea of meeting capital charges from a special tax on land values was also adopted by Canada as far back as 1912. A water corporation was established by legislation to supply water in bulk to the municipalities comprising the greater Winnipeg water district. The public works cost approximately 17,000,000 dollars, and from 1912 to 1927 the whole of the revenue required to pay interest and sinking fund was raised by a special levy on land values—exclusive of improvements—of all the lands within the district (p. 26).

The private provision of infrastructure charges the users, such as by tolls, rentals, and fees. The governmental provision of public goods would best copy what private enterprise does, rather than double bill users by taxing them in addition to their paying higher rentals.

Chapter 5: Time and Interest

1. TIME PREFERENCE

"Interest" is the premium that is paid in order to shift a purchase from the future to the present day. Foundational proposition #14 states that people tend to prefer goods at present to those in the future. This is called "time preference." Given a choice, which would you prefer, $1000 of goods today, or $1000 of goods (adjusted for inflation) thirty years from now?

Most people most of the time would rather have the goods now, for two reasons. First, the human life span is limited, so the sooner one gets something, the more time one will have to enjoy it. Secondly, the future is uncertain, as stated by foundational proposition #15, and we don't know what our situation will be in the future. People also want to buy some products to have them available just in case they need them, even if not for immediate use. People wanting goods now often borrow them, since they don't have the savings to spend to obtain them. When you borrow funds to buy goods with, such as a car or house, instead of waiting until you have saved up enough funds to pay full price, you are shifting the purchase from the future to the present day.

Since future goods are less desired than present ones, they sell at a discount relative to present-day goods. One pays more for present-day goods by paying a premium, which is interest. The rate at which future goods become discounted becomes the natural rate of interest, the interest that would prevail in a pure market. Pure interest based on time preference excludes inflation, risk, and overhead expenses.

We could say, half-jokingly, that interest rates prevent everyone from doing everything at the same time, just as land rent prevents us from wanting to do everything in the same place. The American economist Irving Fisher (1867–1947) built upon the analysis of Menger and Böhm Bawerk in his book *The Theory of Interest* (1930). Fisher explained that greater productivity induces people to shorten their time preference in favor of borrowing more today in order to reap the greater gains, increasing the interest rate. As capital goods accumulate, their increase in productivity becomes reduced, due to diminishing returns, and thus the effect is to lengthen time preferences and reduce interest rates. However, technical progress can offset this by making new types of capital goods, such as computers, more productive.

2. TYPES OF INTEREST RATES

Part of what is called "interest" in the payment for a loan is not really interest, but overhead costs: the labor and other costs of operations of the lender. Another portion of what is called "interest" is really a risk premium, an amount paid to make up for bad debts. There can be a monopoly premium if there are legal restrictions on lending, reducing the supply of loanable funds. After these premia, if there is no inflation, then the depositors of a bank or the owners of the institution receive the remainder, pure interest.

When the money is inflating, part of what is paid to the saver is not pure interest, but makes up for rising prices. The quoted rate, and what is paid in money, is the "nominal rate" of interest. If we subtract the inflation rate from the nominal rate, the "real" rate of interest. It is the real gain, because we have taken out the inflation, leaving the purchasing ability.

The real rate of interest is used in the capitalizing a flow of funds into a stock, or what one would pay to receive that flow. For example, the flow of rent becomes capitalized into the land value. The flow of funds, whether rent or interest or dividends, is divided by the real interest rate to get the value of the stock, or the price of the asset. This assumes that the annual flow is constant. The tax rate on the value of the stock (e.g. price of land) is added to the real interest rate, so that, for example, $p = r / (i + t)$, price equals rent (or other yield) divided by the sum of the interest and tax rates.

The tax rate t can be converted to the tax rate on r as follows: the amount of tax is t^*p, which is divided by r. Since $p = r / (i+t)$, we get $t^*(r/(i+t))/r$. The r cancels out, and we are left with $t/(i+t)$, the tax rate on r. For example, if the tax on land is 20% of the price p and the real interest rate is 5%, then the tax rate on rent is .20 / (.05 + .20) = .20/.25 or 4/5 (80%) of rent.

Capitalization amounts to calculating the present value of a flow of income. At an interest rate of 5%, \$100 invested today will in one year be worth \$105, or 100*1.05. Equivalently, the present value of \$105 is \$105/(1.05) = \$100. Two years from now, \$100 will be worth 100*(1.05)*(1.05), so to calculate the present value, we divide by (1.05)2. In general, the present value of a stream of income is the sum of the incomes for each year, divided by the quantity one plus the interest rate, raised to the power of the number of years into the future.

3. INTEREST RATES, INVESTMENT, AND FACTORS

Suppose you own a firm and have different possibilities for investment. Naturally, you choose those projects with the greatest expected rate of return. But alas, you have no money for investment. No problem, says your financial adviser; we can issue bonds at 8%. The firm will then invest in those projects whose return is greater than 8%.

Interest is usually in the form of money, and it is normally paid on financial capital such as savings accounts in banks, commercial paper (short term borrowing by firms), and bonds. Although the form is money, the substance is goods. By depositing money, you abstain from buying the goods that the money could have bought; when you get money interest, it is a claim on the current stock of goods.

A capital good that does not depreciate can be loaned out indefinitely. The good yields an interest, since funds equal in market value to that good could have been invested as financial capital. But it is an error to call all returns to capital goods interest. As noted in Chapter 4, capital goods depreciate, and the depreciation is a payment for the factors that produced the good, rather than interest.

Since the three factors of production are land, labor, and capital goods, and their returns are rent, wages, and a capital yield, which factor does interest belong to? Interest can be a return to any factor, depending on who does the borrowing. If someone borrows money and buys land, paying the interest on the loan from the rent of the land, then the interest received by the lender is actually rent from that land; hence, some of the interest earned by money in savings accounts which is loaned to landowners is rent. In effect, the lender of the money is the recipient of the rent rather than the nominal owner.

Similarly, if a worker borrows money for his education and pays the interest entirely from his wages, then the return to the lender consists of wages; some of the wages are earned by the worker and are in effect earned by the lender in return for investing in labor improvement, enabling the worker to have improved his skills sooner rather than later. Finally, if the borrowed funds are used to buy capital goods, the return to the lender is part of the yield on those capital goods.

If the loan is for consumption, then the interest paid by the consumer comes from his income from wages, rent, and capital yields, so the interest constitutes those returns earned in part by the lender. For example, if a landowner borrows money for a vacation and then pays it back from his rental income, the recipient of the interest income is getting some of that rent, because that is where the income originated. If all land rent is taxed, then a landowner cannot pay interest on loans from rent, and interest must then come from wages and capital yields. Investment in either better labor or more capital goods would be needed to yield interest. Loans for consumption then reduce the net returns from labor and capital goods of the borrowers, since some of the returns go to the lender. In effect, borrowing to consume now rather than tomorrow reduces your future net returns from your factors, reducing one's future consumption. Likewise, lending to consume tomorrow rather than today increases your future income and consumption.

4. INTEREST AND MONEY, USURY AND ILLUSIONS

Is a high interest rate exploitative? "Usury" is the name for an exploitative rate of return on loans. Sometimes what is seen as a high rate of "interest" for loans is really a risk premium. But exploitation can occur when there is some monopoly leaving borrowers desperate for goods. There can be restrictions on credit and banking, so that the supply of loans is artificially reduced. There can also be laws making it difficult for some people to borrow money; for example, too-liberal bankruptcy laws make personal loans riskier, driving up the risk premium. These exploitative rates on loans are often premiums on monopoly and artificial risks, rather than pure interest due to time preference alone. When pure interest is due to short time preferences, a high desire to consume today rather than tomorrow, it is not exploitative, so it cannot be properly called "usury."

Some people wish to abolish interest because they think it is caused by a money monopoly, since it is an amount paid for the use of money. But, as we have seen, the origin of interest has nothing to do with money, but with time preference. The same interest could also be paid as goods. Money is the medium of loans and borrowings, but goods are the substance.

Interest rates can be analyzed using supply and demand. "Loanable funds" consists of money available to lend. The supply comes from savings and the creation of money. The demand comes from borrowers. The supply curve slopes up, and there is more savings with higher interest rates, and the demand curve slopes down, as more is borrowed with lower rates of interest.

In the short run, interest rates can be affected by changes in the money supply. Suppose the government increases the supply of money. The banks then have more reserves (funds) to loan out. It is as though savings had increased; the supply of loanable funds has gone up. An increase in voluntary savings means time preferences have shifted towards less consumption today and more tomorrow. An increase in the money supply and thus of loanable funds makes interest rates go down, just as they do when savings go up. But real time preferences have not changed. So the added investment is not economically warranted. Too many capital goods, especially of longer duration, will be produced, such as shopping centers and office buildings that stay half empty. The extra money pushes prices up and so the money supply relative to prices goes down to where it was before. Interest rates then go back up to their natural level. So changes in the money supply can make interest rates change in the short run, but not in the long run. In the long run, the natural rate of interest, caused by time preference, will prevail, since an increase in the money supply just raises prices.

Pure interest cannot be abolished, just as rent cannot be. If the government prohibits the payment of interest, then a borrower is in reality receiving the interest—the benefit of present-day use of resources—if he does not need to pay interest, just as tenants of land receive the land rent if they do not need to pay it to others. If banks share in the profits from enterprises that borrow funds rather than directly charging interest (a practice in Islamic banking), then this bank share is implicitly interest whether one wishes to label it so or not.

Another illusion is the notion that interest creates inflation because more money is needed to pay back a loan, that if you borrow $100 and pay back $110, we need $10 more in cash, creating inflation. But if the loan is for current consumption, the interest is paid by the borrower's reduced future consumption; he must in the future consume less in order to also pay back the loan. No new money is needed. One person is paying interest and another receiving it; so the net demand for cash is the same. If the loan is for investment, the interest is normally paid from the increase in productivity and output.

We see, then, that pure interest does not exploit any factor of production. What does cause economic problems is the distortion of natural interest rates and the increase of premiums by government interventions, whether directly, in the form of interest-rate controls, or indirectly by money creation, banking monopolies, the government's money monopoly, and restrictions on credit, which force desperate people to borrow at high rates in order to survive. Poor people with bad credit, for example, may have to borrow money at high rates from loan sharks; this is not pure interest but a premium for high risk and money and credit monopolies (the restriction of credit due to loose bankruptcy laws and financial restrictions). Also, small businesses are often forced to borrow funds because regulations make it too expensive for them to issue shares of stock.

In a pure market economy, with no restrictions on honest and peaceful money, banking, or lending, interest rates simply ration goods over time between future and present-day uses, enabling those who most urgently want to consume or produce today to do so at a price that reflects preferences over time.

Chapter 6: Consumption and Demand

1. WHAT HAPPENS TO INCOME?

What happens to income? It can either be used for consumption, to buy goods and services, or the income can be saved. Savings are usually put in a bank or other financial institution, which loans it out to borrowers who spend. One can directly invest one's income for capital goods or for human capital. If your investment is direct, such as buying a car, you are getting an implicit return. If you instead had to borrow a car, you would be paying the owner a periodic fee; so if you own your own car, you are paying the yield to yourself, just like if you own land, it has a rent regardless of whether any explicit or money payments are being made.

Another way of spending income is to waste it. Waste involves the use of resources in different ways than the owners would have wanted, and without benefit to them. If a vandal destroys your car, for example, this is not only your own loss, but a social loss as well, since this resource has been wasted. If the government builds a road in a forest that benefits only a few individuals (say, the owners of a lumber company), then the wealth of the original owners has been wasted, used in ways they would not desire and do not benefit from. This road is not a true investment, since its yield is less than what investors would get in a free market. Government subsidies are usually wasteful, and costs imposed by government restrictions and taxes are also a social waste of resources, since they not only extract funds that people would want to spend in different ways, the interventions can also make resources such as labor idle, i.e. unemployed.

2. CONSUMERS' UTILITY

What, then, determines how income is consumed? Let's go back to the foundational premises of economics in Chapter 1. Proposition #8 states that human beings have ends, or goals, desires, and needs. Proposition #11 states that human values, and thus these ends, are subjective. Proposition #9 states that people are able to rank their ends into those of greater and lesser importance.

The theory of economic values was pioneered by the founder of the Austrian school of economic thought, Carl Menger (1871). He defined value as "the importance that individual goods or quantities of goods attain for us because we are conscious of being dependent on command of them for the satisfaction of our needs" (p. 115). Values are thus subjective, since each individual perceives the importance of goods from his own needs or desires, from his own feelings and thoughts. Value originates in the human mind rather than in things: "Value is thus nothing inherent in goods" (p. 120). We know from experience that what pleases one person will be detested by another person.

Goods have utility, or usefulness and importance, because we value them. As Menger stated it, "Utility is the capacity of a thing to serve for the satisfaction of human needs" (p. 119). In ranking our subjective ends or desires, we also rank the desirability or utility of the various goods that have the capacity to satisfy these desires.

Menger then notes that "these differences in the importance of different satisfactions can be observed not only with the satisfaction of needs of different kinds but also with the more or less complete satisfaction of one and the same need" (pp. 123–4). For example, you not only desire food, but a different amounts for different reasons, such as for survival, health, or enjoyment. The highest rank might be for survival, then for health, and then for enjoyment, or perhaps some folks would rank enjoyment greater than health, as we often do some of the time. Hence, we rank food-value in terms of the decreasing importance of various amounts. In general, for any good, different amounts satisfy different types of needs or desires of different importance, so that as we consume ever more of it, ever decreasing desires are satisfied, until the amount is reached when, at some moment, "a more complete satisfaction of that particular need is a matter of indifference" (p. 125). Even more consumption would then become a burden.

So the utility derived from some good diminishes as you obtain more and more of it. Maybe the first small increments give increasing utility, but eventually the utility of increasing amounts diminishes. This is called "diminishing marginal utility."

The marginal utility, the value you place on an extra amount of a good, depends on the subjective importance or value of only that extra amount, regardless of the value of the previous amounts. So what you would be willing to pay for that amount depends only on that marginal or extra utility obtained, not on the utility of the previous amounts. And here is the kicker: when you buy a certain amount of a good, if all the units of the goods (like individual oranges in a bag) are priced identically, then the price you are willing to pay per unit depends on the utility of the last, the marginal, the least important unit. Otherwise, you would not buy that extra or last unit!

For example, if apples and oranges are each priced at 20 cents each, but you prefer oranges to apples, you would rather buy one orange than one apple. You value the second orange (at that moment) less than the first, but still greater than the apple. But now, having two oranges, you would rather have one apple than a third orange. If oranges are priced cheaply, you'll then take a fourth or fifth one. You don't want an extra apple because an extra orange is more important at the time. But if that day oranges are expensive, then you might only take two, plus one apple, since the first couple of oranges are more important and valued than the next few. So the price you are willing to pay for one orange or one apple depends on the value to you of that last apple or orange taken, rather than the first.

As Menger put it, "The value of a particular good ... is thus for [an individual] equal to the importance of the least important of the satisfactions assured by the whole quantity available" (p. 139). Marginal utility explains why water is so cheap where it is in large supply, even though it is an important commodity overall. When lots of water is available, the last unit you buy will be put to a relatively unimportant use, like washing your car. The marginal value of water, then, is low, even though some of the water (the first amounts you would buy if it were scarcer) is very important.

The consumer optimum is the amount of goods for which the marginal utility of each good relative to the price is equal for all goods. If the marginal utility of one good, relative to the price, is higher than for other goods, the consumer is better off buying more of that good, until its marginal utility has diminished so that its MU/P is equal to that of all other goods. In that case, the last dollar or pound spent on all goods give the same amount of marginal utility, and you can't do any better.

3. THE LAW OF DEMAND

To "demand" in economics does not mean to boldly and angrily insist on getting something, but simply to both want something and be able to pay for it. A demand for a product means the quantities that consumers are willing and able to buy at various prices. Because of diminishing marginal utility, people buy more of a good if the price is less, since they will be willing to satisfy less important desires if the price is lower.

The price of a good is not just the amount one has to pay for something, but also the foregone opportunities. If you spend $100 for a coat, you have lost the opportunity to spend that amount on something else. The real cost is therefore the foregone opportunities, not the $100, since that $100 will be spent on something. At a lower price, the foregone opportunities are fewer or less valuable. This concept of cost being a foregone opportunity is called "opportunity cost," another concept pioneered by the Austrian school, namely by Friedrich von Wieser.

Land has an opportunity cost for an individual, but for an economy as a whole, the land is already there, so there is no opportunity cost in its use overall (as opposed to use for a particular purpose). Labor does have an opportunity cost because the alternative is leisure. Thus, for any good, at different prices there are different opportunity costs, and the lower the price, the lower these costs, relative to the subjective value of another unit of a good. Hence, there is a relationship between different prices of a good and the amount one is willing to buy: the lower the price, the more one is willing to forego other opportunities and buy another unit of the good.

When the price of a good falls, the quantity purchased can increase for two reasons. One is the substitution effect, in which people substitute the cheaper goods for the now more expensive other goods. The second reason is the income effect, since lower prices provide a greater purchasing power, so people buy more stuff.

A demand function consists of the various quantities of a good demanded for each price of a good. We can mathematically describe this function as $Q = f(P)$; quantity bought is a function of price. The actual relationship for various values of the function can be written in a schedule or table, or plotted in a graph. Such a graph has price along the vertical axis, the opposite from the normal mathematical convention of having the independent variable on the horizontal, thanks to Alfred Marshall (1842–1924), the economist who pioneered the analysis of supply and demand. Quantity is then on the horizontal axis, and we then draw points showing the quantities demanded for each of various possible prices. These points are then jointed together to form a "demand curve." You can search for "demand curve" in the Internet for graphic examples.

Since a greater quantity is demanded at a lower price, a demand curve slopes down, diagonally to the right. This is called the "law of demand," a fundamental principle of economics. As we have seen, the law of demand is derived from the diminishing marginal utility for increasing amounts of consumer goods. Demand curves can also be horizontal (where the price is always the same) or vertical (where the quantity is fixed regardless of price, such as for urgently needed medicine). The law of demand states that the quantity demanded does not increase with higher prices.

The quantity of goods demanded can be of two types. For flows, goods in continuous production and consumption, the quantity is an amount per unit of time. For example, the demand for oranges is a certain amount per week or month. The quantity axis is then Q/T, quantity per time interval.

The other type of good is a stock, a certain quantity at one moment of time. For example, the demand for a certain rare stamp is that of a stock. No more of these stamps are being produced; there is no flow of product. Instead, collectors bid already-existing stamps from one another, competing for a fixed stock. At any moment in time, there will be bids and offers for stamps, and an exchange takes place when a bid and offer match in price. The demand for the stamps are therefore the number of bids at any particular moment in time at some price. At a higher price, fewer collectors are willing to bid for a stamp. So the demand curve for stocks of goods also slopes down, but the quantity axis is for bids at a certain moment. The market for land is such a market, since people bid for existing parcels, buying from a previous owner rather than for newly manufactured or imported land.

The demand for consumer goods depends of many variables, such as subjective preferences (or tastes), income and wealth, and alternative goods and prices. The demand curve for a good for an entire economy is simply the addition of all the demand curves of the individuals.

A "change in demand" is a shift of the entire demand curve, or a change of the quantities at all the prices. If there is only a change in price, we move along the demand curve or schedule to the quantity demanded at that price. When an economist talks about an "increase in demand," the meaning is that there has been a shift in the demand curve towards greater quantities at all prices.

4. ELASTICITY OR RESPONSIVENESS

An entrepreneur wishes to know how much more of his product will be bought if he lowers or increases the price. What he wants to know is called the "price elasticity of demand." We can blame Alfred Marshall for this confusing terminology, just as he is to blame for switching the demand-curve axes. A better term for elasticity would be "responsiveness." The price elasticity is the responsiveness of the quantity demanded to a small change in the price of a good. It is measured as the proportionate (or percentage) change in quantity divided by the proportionate change in price. The technical calculation is as follows: (change in quantity/quantity)/(change in price/price). By convention economists often use the absolute value of the ratio.

Demand is said to be elastic if the price elasticity (quantity responsiveness) is high. This means a small change in price leads to a relatively large change in quantity demanded. Demand is called elastic if its value is greater than one, which means the proportionate change in quantity is greater than in price.

The opposite is an inelastic demand, if the quantity responsiveness is low, less than 1. If it is exactly 1, then it has "unitary elasticity" or is "unit elastic." These elasticities are important in applied economics, since enterprises want to know the effects of price changes, and they experiment to see what the quantity responsiveness is.

There are two other elasticities relevant to demand. One is (again confusingly called) the "income elasticity of demand," which would be better called the "quantity responsiveness to income." Here, we measure the change in quantity demanded when there is a change in income. This is calculated as the percentage change in quantity divided by a percentage change in income—this time keeping the positive or negative sign. If we expect incomes to rise, an enterprise wants to know how the demand curve for his product will shift.

A third type is the "cross elasticity of demand," which means, in English, the responsiveness of the quantity demanded of one good when the price of another good changes. It is calculated as the percentage change in quantity for one good divided by the percentage change in price for another good. This cross-price elasticity is important in being able to tell which goods are substitutes and which are complements.

A good is a substitute for another if one can switch from one to the other without much loss in utility. For example, if you don't much care whether your pencil is colored yellow or blue on the outside, they are close substitutes. We can measure this with the cross-price elasticity. If it is positive, the goods are substitutes, because it means an increase in the price of one good (blue pencils) induce an increase in quantity demanded in another good (yellow pencils). A big increase in the price of green apples would likely lead to people buying less of them and more of its substitute, red apples.

If the cross price elasticity is negative, the goods are complements. A complement is a good that is used together with another one. For example, your left shoe is a complement to your right one. Suppose they were sold separately, and the price of right shoes went way up. You would not only buy fewer right shoes, but also fewer left ones, since you want both together. The cross price elasticity would be negative, since an increase in the price of left shoes leads to a decrease in quantity bought of right shoes. If the cross price elasticity is zero, then there is no relationship between the two goods.

5. CONSUMER DEMAND AND THE FACTORS OF PRODUCTION

In our model in Chapter 3 on rent, we had only one crop, corn, and the rent and wages were calculated in terms of corn. But in a complex economy with many goods, which goods determine the value of wages and rent?

We again turn to Menger. We have seen that the values of consumer goods are subjective. As you recall from Chapter 4, capital goods are called by Menger "goods of higher order" than consumer goods. As Menger put it, "the value of goods of higher order is always and without exception determined by the prospective value of the goods of lower order in whose production they serve" (p. 150). In other words, if consumers value corn highly relative to other goods, then the goods of higher order used to produce those of lower order will have value. Land and labor used in growing corn have value because corn has value. The value of corn is not due to the costs of growing it; on the contrary, the resources used in growing it have value because the product has value. If you worked all day making mud pies, your labor would have a value of nil, if no one would want that product (unless your mother bought some).

As Menger recognized, the determination of the factors land and labor from the expected value of their final products is consistent with the law of rent, as analyzed in Chapter 3: "The existence of the special characteristics that land and the services of land … exhibit is by no means denied. In any country, land is usually available only in quantities that cannot be easily increased; it is fixed as to situation; and it has an extraordinary variety of grades" (p. 169). Menger's theory deepens our insight into why land and labor have value at all. It was because the corn had value that the differential rent appeared in the first place and that the wages paid in corn had any value. But it is not the value of corn alone that would determine the rent of a particular lot of land.

As Menger wrote (p. 169), a factor of production will also have a greater value if complementary factors have a smaller value. Suppose that we need irrigation in order to use a particular area of land. If this water is cheap, then land rent will be higher than if the irrigation is more expensive.

6. COST-INFLUENCED CHOICE

Building upon the theory of subjective values, James Buchanan (1969), a pioneer of public choice theory which uses economics to analyze government, also developed the theory of choice. If you are choosing among goods with your own money, your choice will be "cost influenced," since each choice has an opportunity cost of foregone alternatives. Recall in the beginning of the chapter that we had three categories of spending: consumption, investment, and waste. Consumption is a cost-influenced choice. Some government spending is equivalent to cost-influenced consumption and investment, since the taxpayers would, if given a direct choice over their funds, want to buy some of the things government buys, such as perhaps highways and wildlife conservation. But some of government spending will not have been so chosen.

An individual may choose to buy an item he later regrets having bought. In retrospect, it was a waste. But since he did not know this beforehand, the spending is wasted. The key is whether the choice is cost-influenced. If at the moment of choice, you bear the cost and make a free choice, then the item bought is in the category of consumption or investment. The relevant utility of an item is that which is made at the very moment of choice. The fact that you might later have buyer's remorse is irrelevant so far as the consumption is concerned. It's too late. The spending is now a sunk cost. Economics looks forwards to the future. Prices are always based on the expected utilities, not on the actual utility once a choice has been made. The past is important in influencing the future. A bad product will not be bought much in the future, if the word gets around. The past guides our future, but our expectations about the future determine our utilities and therefore the prices of goods.

Chapter 7: Production and Profit

1. THE THREE SECTORS OF AN ECONOMY

Having analyzed consumption, we turn now to production. We already have seen how production uses three factors, land, labor, and capital goods. We can now examine the second dimension of an economy, its three sectors: household, firms, and government. The third dimension was described in Chapter 5, the categories of expenditure as consumption and investment.

Households consist of individuals, families, and other living-together arrangements, such as room mates and communes. Firms are the organizations which engage in the production of wealth. Government is the agency that has authority and power over the rules that firms and households are legally required to abide by in their consumption and production.

All wealth is owned by households. They either own firms personally or own shares in corporations. Households who are citizens are the ultimate owners of the land of a country and of its government's wealth. As owners, households rent their factors to firms, hiring themselves to firms as workers, loaning firms their capital goods, and renting land to firms. Firms may, of course, nominally (in name) own resources, but the ultimate owners are households.

Households obtain an income from loaning the factors to firms, and they use this income to invest in capital goods (for firms or government) and for consumption. Households are thus the sector that consumes the wealth produced by the firms.

Firms can be generally divided into four types: 1) families; 2) for-profit firms; 3) non-profit organizations; 4) government enterprises. Non-profit organizations include churches and foundations. The motivation of for-profit firms is normally to maximize profits, but the ultimate goal is the maximization of utility, which can also involve achieving a large size of firm or getting prestige.

For-profit firms in turn have various possible forms of organization. The simplest is a single proprietorship, where an individual owns the firm. Next in complexity is a partnership, owned by several persons. A family is one possible partnership; it engages in household production, such as gardening. A marriage is also a partnership.

Most complex are corporations, firms whose owners have shares of stock and elect a board of directors to operate the firm. Typically, the board hires a president or manager. A corporation may take the form of a cooperative, in which a shareholder is also a member, and each member has one vote regardless of shares. Another form is a non-stock corporation, such as condominium housing, in which the owners are members and have various types of voting rights, but where ownership consists of having title to units, like apartments, which are tied into the membership of the firm.

In many countries, corporations have legally limited liability, which means that the ordinary shareholders may not be liable for debts of the company beyond the value of their shares. The board, though, is usually liable for the debt beyond their shares in the company. A disadvantage of corporations in the U.S. is that corporate income is taxed twice, once when the corporation earns it, and secondly when it distributes dividends to the shareholders, which is taxed again as personal income.

An advantage of corporations with shares of stock is that the shares trade on active exchange markets, so an investment in the corporation is highly "liquid," and also divisible. This enables a corporation to raise large amounts of money by issuing stock.

A problem with corporations is that the management may seek to promote its own well-being rather than that of the share holders. This is resolved by means of profit-sharing methods of payment as well as managers competing for their positions and the possibility of a takeover if a firm becomes too fat with management benefits.

Besides stocks and units of ownership, companies can also issue debt in the form of bonds. These pay interest for a certain period of time, after which the bond "matures" and the company takes them back and pays back the principal.

The agents who organize the factors of production are called the entrepreneurs. Often they are owners of firms or executives with a great deal of control, but sometimes they can be sales persons or anyone that is able to organize production. Entrepreneurs are the drivers of a market economy; they actively seek out opportunities to bring resources to a more productive use, such as by developing new products or new methods, or bringing goods to markets they were not previously available in. If you have a vegetable garden in your back yard, you too are an entrepreneur, since you decide what to grow, how to grow it, and who gets the produce.

Government plays three different roles. First, some of its agencies act as firms. Governments run enterprises such as the post office, railroads, and street maintenance. In this role, government is a firm hiring factors and producing wealth. So part of government is also in the category of firms. Governments also issue bonds, but not shares of stock.

Secondly, government enacts rules that must be followed by the three sectors (including itself). These rules are of two types: 1) rules creating markets, and 2) rules that intervene or interfere in markets. The distinction follows the universal ethic developed in Chapter 1. Rules which coerce households and firms, which impose costs or restrictions, i.e. any rule other than prohibiting and penalizing coercive harm to others, are interventions. Subsidies are also interventions. It is not claimed here that interventions are bad; those who advocate them claim that the benefits exceed the cost.

Other rules create and maintain markets. For example, uniform and constant rules protecting property rights and enforcing contracts enable markets to operate efficiently. Laws setting up copyrights make a market in literature and art more efficient, preventing publishers from having to write a contract with each buyer regarding copying of the books. Laws setting up patents also simplify transaction costs, also preventing firms from having to write complex contracts with each user of the firm to avoid copying, and making the enforcement easier. Some people feel that copyrights and patents create monopolies and are thus inefficient, while others are of the view that patents and copyrights are general contracts between the sellers and buyers of new products, without which the new products might not be created or written.

The third function of government is redistribution. Governments typically take much of the wealth from the first and second distributions (see Chapter 5) and forcefully redistributes it to others. Hence, much consumption is done by recipients of redistributed income who have not earned it by supplying factors to firms.

There is another agent in the economy, the thief. A thief also performs forced redistribution, taking wealth and income by force. Their redistribution is not legally sanctioned; they impose their own independent rules and redistribution.

There are two circular flows in the economy among the sectors, for goods and money. Goods, produced by firms (including government firms), flow to households and to government. In turn, households supply factor resources to firms and government.

The second flow, money, circulates in the opposite direction, since a consumer obtains goods in exchange for money. Firms pay money to households and to government for the use of factors. Households and government then use the money to pay the firms (including government) for goods, or lose some money to thieves, or pay taxes to government.

2. THE PRODUCTION POSSIBILITIES CURVE

When we disaggregate wealth into various products, the question arises as to how much of each is to be produced. We begin the analysis with a simple economy with only two products, bread and lettuce. The economy could produce only bread or only lettuce or some of each. Suppose that only bread is being produced, for a total of 100 loaves. Now we want to produce ten heads of lettuce. If the economy was fully employed in making the 100 loaves, some resources must be taken away from bread making to make the lettuce.

To analyze the economics of the trade-off between the two products, we again begin with the foundational principles. Proposition #1 states that some natural resources are scarce. So there is a finite amount of land and labor available in an economy, which is why only so much bread or lettuce can be produced, and not enough to satisfy everyone if they were free. Proposition #2 states that resources vary in quality, and proposition #4 tells us that different amounts of inputs will produce different amounts of outputs. Applying this, we see that some land is more productively used to grow wheat for bread, while other land is more productively used to grow lettuce; and likewise some labor has been trained to grow wheat and bake bread while other labor has been educated in growing lettuce. Then capital goods, of course, have been made specializing in one or the other.

When we use a bit less land, labor, and capital goods to produce bread and use it to make lettuce, how do we do this? Proposition #12 states that people economize. So we economize by giving up that wheat-growing land that is most suitable for growing lettuce, as well as labor, etc., that was trained to grow nice lettuce. Likewise, if we had been growing only lettuce, the most productive resources would be used to grow the first increment of wheat and to bake bread. The next most productive resources will be used to produce the next increments of the products.

If we then plot all combinations of bread and lettuce that can be produced, we get a curve. We have bread on one axis and lettuce on the other axis, and for each amount of bread, there is a certain maximum amount of lettuce that can be grown. This is the "production possibilities curve," PPC.

This curve demonstrates several principles. First is the principle of efficiency. Production is efficient if the total product is on the PPC. If the total output lies within the PPC, then one or more of the products can be increased without decreasing the other; hence, society is not producing efficiently. Efficient production means that the production of any product cannot be increased without reducing the amount of any other product. The existence of waste, of course, implies that society is inside the PPC relative to the desires of those obtaining the income of the first two distributions.

A second principle is opportunity cost. To produce more bread, we must produce less lettuce; the opportunity cost of producing more bread is less lettuce.

The third principle is the "law of increasing cost." Economizing persons use the most productive resources first. Increased amounts of the good will require less productive resources, resources which may be used more productively in other uses. So the law of increasing cost states that as we increase the production of one good, the opportunity cost of foregone production of other goods tends to increase. Therefore, the shape of the PPC is "bowed out," like a rainbow. Economists say it is "concave to the origin," but you can just think of it as bowed out unless you want to impress your friends. The curve is bowed because at first, giving up a little wheat gets you a lot of that first amount of lettuce, and vice versa.

The effect of better technology is to push out the whole PPC outwards, so that the same amounts of inputs yields a greater amount of output. The effect of accumulating more capital goods is also to push out the PPC, since land and labor become more productive. There is therefore a trade-off between consuming now and consuming tomorrow. We can consume less today and invest in new capital goods in order to consume more tomorrow.

3. THE PRODUCTION FUNCTION

Since a firm, in abstract, is an organization inputting resources and outputting products, we can describe it as a production function, or a product as a function of inputs. A function is a relationship between a dependent variable and some independent variables. The inputs are the independent variables, and output is dependent. The relationship can be concisely stated as $Q/T = f(N,L,K)$, where Q/T is output per time interval, N is the number and quality of workers, L is the amount and quality of land, and K represents capital goods. Note that these are all physical inputs and output; there is no financial capital such as money in the function.

The methods of production, the technology and rules (including government regulations, the role of luck, and the goals of the firm owners) are included in the functional variable f.

We can see then that if the amount of a resource such as N, labor, is varied, output will vary. The marginal product of labor is in fact the change in output Q/T caused by a change in labor, N.

In order to maximize profits, costs must be minimized, and this implies that the amount of each input will be determined by its marginal product, proportional to its cost. In the cost-minimizing combination of inputs, the marginal productivity of a dollar's worth of all inputs must be the same. If the marginal product of one input, divided by price, is lower than that of another, then costs can be reduced by switching, if possible, to the inputs with the higher relative productivity.

4. THE THEORY OF EXCHANGE

Some people have the idea that agriculture or manufacturing is "productive," but trading, buying goods in one place and selling in another, or exchanging one good for another among two persons, is not productive, but just moves things around. But Menger showed that this is not so.

Menger showed how in an exchange of goods, the goods have unequal rather than equal subjective value. They may have an equal market value, but the subjective values must be different, otherwise the trade would not take place. Trade only takes place if person A has some good that is of less value to him than some good that B has.

Using Menger's (1871, p. 183) example, suppose A has horses and B has cows. Because of diminishing marginal utility, each extra horse has less and less value to A, and so with cows for B. Suppose the first cow or horse has a value of 50 to A and B, and that each extra one has a value of 10 less than the previous. Then if A has 5 horses, the fifth is only worth 10 to him. But it would be worth 50 to B. Same with cows. So they trade. A now has 4 horses and 1 cow. He lost 10 of value by giving up the horse, and gained 50 by getting the cow, for a net gain of 40. Likewise, B has a net gain of 40 from getting a horse.

As Menger states (p. 184), "each of the two traders obtained an economic gain from this first exchange equivalent to the gain that would accrue to him if his wealth had been increased by a good whose value to him is equal to 40… Trade is therefore no less productive than industrial or agricultural activity." Economic exchange contributes to consumers' utility and thus an increase in the subjective value of their wealth just as effectively as the physical increase of more goods. As Menger stated, "the end of economy is not the physical augmentation of goods but always the fullest satisfaction of human needs" (p. 190).

Both will continue to exchange as long as the marginal utility of the other's good is greater than that of the goods they have. The next horse or cow has a marginal utility of 20 to the owner and 40 to the other, so they exchange, each increasing utility by 20. After that, the marginal utilities are 30 for both, so they stop trading. Note that once the goods are of equal marginal value, trade comes to a halt. Trade went on because of unequal rather than equal subjective marginal values.

An important principle of exchange is that trade will continue until the economic gains, the gains from trade, are exhausted, until the marginal values of what one has is equal or greater than what others have.

5. SUPPLY CURVES

We derived demand curves in Chapter 5, and now we will derive supply curves, the supply of goods offered by firms.

A market supply is the quantities of goods that a producer is willing to produce and sell at particular prices. Like demand, the quantity is a function of (dependent on) price, but the quantity axis is horizontal and the price is on the vertical axis, by the convention set by Alfred Marshall.

Like demand schedules or curves, a supply can either be a flow, or quantity produced during some time interval, or a stock, a certain amount of goods at one particular moment in time.

The amount of goods competitive firms are willing to supply at various prices depends on the costs of production. Costs in the short run are either fixed or variable, fixed costs being those which cannot be changed during that time interval. In the long run, all costs can be changed; indeed, the "long run" is defined for any particular firm as that time interval at which all costs are variable.

Average costs are simply total costs divided by the number of units, while marginal cost is the cost of producing one more unit (or tiny amount of product). A firm obtains a maximum profit when total revenues are greater than total costs and its marginal cost just equals its marginal revenue, since any extra unit would cost more than it gets in revenues. If the long-term average cost is greater than the price, then the firm will shut down, unless the owners enjoy taking losses.

While demand curves slope down, supply curves slope up for produced goods, while, as noted in Chapter 3 on land, the supply curve for land as space is vertical, as is the supply curve for goods no longer in production, like rare coins and stamps, or old art.

Supply curves, for goods being produced, slope up diagonally due to the universal propositions about physical resources. Inputs are scarce, and some locations are more productively devoted to one use than another, relative to the values placed on them by consumers. So to increase the amount of bread, as we saw, land use must be drawn away from the production of lettuce, which may not be as productive for bread as the use devoted to bread. So the relative price of the new inputs is higher. Some locations, such as city centers, generate more output per unit of area than others, so the cost per unit of output is lower. If the output units sell at one price, then a higher price is need to engage the less productive locations. Greater quantities are produced only if the price fetched in the market is higher, and the supply curve slopes up.

Short-run marginal costs increase as the marginal product of variable factors declines, since some of the inputs such as land are fixed during that time. However, over the long run, this tendency of input prices to increase can be offset by a change in f, the technology and method of production. At greater amounts of production, in some industries, more efficient ways of producing can be achieved. For example, it is more expensive to make a few cars than to mass-produce them in huge factories. There can be physical reasons for long-run economies of scale; the volume of facilities such as pipes and buildings increase at a greater rate than their surfaces, so the per-unit volume costs can go down with larger structures.

This is called "economies of scale." Unit or average costs decrease with greater production. So an industry with such economies of scale will have a downward-sloping long-run average cost curve until economies from greater scale are exhausted, after which the firm has constant returns to scale. With an even larger scale, there can be diseconomies or increasing average costs of managing an ever larger firm, as management gets more and more complicated and eats up a bigger portion of costs, so at a very large scale, the long-run average cost would go up again.

It is also possible for the supply curve to be horizontal, if the costs of inputs are the same at all levels of production and there are no economies of scale. This is called a "constant cost" industry.

If the average cost of firm output first decreases and then increases, in a U-shaped curve, then the marginal cost curve must cross it at its lowest point, the marginal costs first pulling down and then pulling up the average.

Just as we distinguish a shift in a demand curve from a movement along a demand curve, we distinguish a shift in the supply curve (a change in the quantity supplied at all prices) from a movement along a supply curve (a change in quantity supplied as the price of a product changes). A decrease in government regulations or improvement in technology, for example, would shift a supply curve out, making it possible to produce more for any particular price.

6. PRICE EQUILIBRIUM

Now that we have the two sides of the market, demand and supply, we can join the two curves in one graph. As the demand curve slopes down, it will typically intersect the supply curve. The point where the curves intersect determines the market price and quantity at that time.

It is quite possible that the curves will not intersect at all. You offer a poem on the market for only a dollar, but the demand curve starts at 25 cents for one poem and slopes down to 100 copies of the poem demanded if it is free. But your supply curve began at $1 for the first poem; you refuse to sell it for any less, so the curves do not intersect. The quantity exchanged in that case is zero.

If the curves do intersect, then economists call the price and quantity an "equilibrium." An equilibrium at a moment in time is a situation in which the gains from trade have become exhausted. If there were a shortage, gains from trade would be possible as sellers increased the price to buyers willing to pay more to get the goods. If there is a glut or surplus of goods, gains from trade can be made as sellers lower the price to get rid of the stuff. Either would be called a disequilibrium, since gains from trading can still be made. At equilibrium, trade halts, because gains from trade have become exhausted.

But wait a minute! If trade stops, then how can there be a market equilibrium price? Is this a paradox? The answer is that at each moment, markets are moving towards equilibrium, but never actually reach it (or if they do in limited situations, trade stops). People eat; they are in equilibrium and stop eating. Then they get hungry again, in disequilibrium, and go to market. They bid for food, while sellers make offers. The market price attains an equilibrium price as gains from trade are exhausted, but then hungry new buyers in disequilibrium keep coming afterwards, making new bids.

Hence, a market price constantly equilibrates or matches demands and supplies, and does not grind to a halt. This equilibrating clears the market—sellers are matched by buyers at the current price—but new buyers and sellers are always dynamically making bids and offers. Just because the price is stable does not mean equilibrium (in each moment) has been achieved. It just means that bids and offers are somewhat constant during some time interval. The price is always subject to change if there is some change in the amounts and flows of bids or offers. Of course if we consider a time range greater than a moment, then, looking back in time, we observe that often there is some narrow price range in which exchanges have taken place, and we can consider that to be a equilibrium during that duration.

7. PROFIT

The term "profit" is used in different ways by accountants and economists. To an accountant, profit is the difference between explicit or money revenues and money costs. An economist subtracts from this profit the implicit costs of a firm. Suppose a farmer owns his own land, which he could rent for $10,000 per year. An accountant says his profit was $50,000 that year. But the farmer could have rented his land out for $10,000; by not doing so, he lost $10,000 in potential revenue. This is an opportunity cost of using the land himself. Since the land rent is a cost regardless of to whom it is paid, an economist subtracts it as an implicit cost, not paid in money but a cost of using that factor nevertheless. So the economic profit is reduced to $40,000. But wait: the farmer's own wages must be subtracted too. If he could have earned $30,000 working for someone else, that too is an implicit cost, a wage. So we have $10,000 left. But what about the capital goods? He could have hired them out for $6,000 that year. Subtract this implicit yield on capital goods, and we are left with a $4,000 economic profit. This is also called an entrepreneurial profit.

But since wealth is divided into a first distribution of wages, rent, and capital yields, where does this economic profit fit in? Since entrepreneurs are also workers, this entrepreneurial profit is really a type of wage.

But it is a special type of wage. Foundational proposition #15 states that the future is uncertain. Entrepreneurs are innovators, but they can't be sure whether they will earn a profit from trying or organize factors in what they expect to be better ways. Uncertainty cannot be insured against, unlike ordinary risk. Normal risks such as fires occur with some regularity in a larger-number environment, and insurance companies can measure how much loss there has been in an average year and provide insurance against it. But, as economist Frank Knight pointed out, uncertainty does not have probability distributions. New products are unique in time and circumstance, we cannot know what the probability of success is. So entrepreneurs and their fellow investors take a chance, and if they are right, their reward is entrepreneurial or economic profits. If they are wrong, they take losses.

Profits and losses are important signals in a market economy. Consistently high profits in an industry indicate that more resources can be devoted to this product. Losses indicate that too much production has taken place in that industry. Taxes on profits skew these signals, reducing the potential investment and entrepreneurship in an economy, reducing output, efficiency, and employment.

We see then, that profits induce firms to produce, innovate, and employ factors. How this is done by the economy as a whole will be the subject of the next chapter.

Chapter 8: Industrial Organization

1. HOW MARKETS WORK

In order to understand the concept of a market, it is helpful to look at its evolution.

Trade may have begun with informal agreements among neighbors, such as the basket-weaver offering his handiwork to the farmer next door, in exchange for some of the farmer's fresh vegetables. But, in time, trade became carried out on a more community-wide basis—in particular gathering spots called markets. Today, we use the term "market economy" to refer to a society where people meet their needs through voluntary agreements of exchange. A "market" is not a particular place or group of people, but the process of voluntary production, exchange, distribution, and consumption.

Initially, trade was carried on through barter—the direct exchange of one good for another. However, for large-scale trading, barter is a cumbersome business: any farmer, for example, who wants to swap his vegetables for some tools, needs not only to find someone willing to trade in tools, but to trade tools specifically for vegetables. Trade through barter requires what is called "a double coincidence of wants."

The story of how traders solved this problem has been related by many authors, Menger (1871, p. 258) having analyzed it in detail. As related by Menger, although barter limited the exchanges of traders, "there were elements in their situation that everywhere led men inevitably, without the need for a special agreement or even government compulsion, to a state of affairs in which this difficulty was completely overcome. Traders realized that they could exchange their specialized products for commodities which had a greater marketability, which they could then trade for what they wanted to consume." Cattle, for example, were readily saleable in many areas.

And so, in any particular market area, certain goods, such as cattle, cocoa beans, gold, or wampum, became intermediate goods with exchange value, and the use of such goods for payments became a social custom. Menger emphasizes the importance of custom, since "the actual performance of exchange operations of this kind presupposes a knowledge of their interest on the part of economizing individuals" (p. 261).

Money eliminated the need for the more cumbersome system of bartering, but whether one is trading with money or through barter, the act of voluntary exchange is what creates a market. As defined in Chapter 1, a "market" is the totality of voluntary economic acts in some context. The term market denotes anything from an exchange between two individuals on a street corner, to the more elaborate trading on Wall Street. A market process cannot be perceived as detached from the people who create it.

Classical economists noted that a free market will allocate scarce resources effectively without the need for any central direction. The output produced is generally the amount that people wanted to buy, without severe shortages or surpluses. How is it that production manages to adjust to the continually changing wants of consumers?

Markets are able to allocate resources through the price system. Prices serve as a signal to a consumer about the relative costs of goods, which they compare to their subjective valuations of these goods. Prices also indicate the costs and revenues to producers. Consumers and producers react to prices in their buying and selling decisions, determining the types and quantities of products.

If more of one item—a hammer for instance—is demanded, hammers become sold out. There is a temporary shortage. This will cause the price of a hammer to rise, eliminating the shortage. But then since producers are making a greater profit, this stimulates them to produce more hammers. As more hammers are supplied, the price of hammers will go down again, though perhaps not to the previous level, since it may cost more to draw resources from other uses in order to make more hammers. And so the market ends up with more hammers, perhaps at a bit higher price, equilibrating the desires of consumers with the costs of producers.

Similarly, imagine that too much of a certain commodity, such as coffee, has been supplied. Through competition among sellers to get rid of their coffee, the price will be pushed down. But at the lower price there is less profit, so producers will reduce their supply, thereby reducing the glut of coffee.

So we can see that through an enormous system of trial and error the price system will ultimately balance supply with demand—fluctuating prices will ensure that a glut or shortage of an item or service does not persist.

Adam Smith, in his classic text *The Wealth of Nations*, praised the workings of the price system. He demonstrated how through the price system, the an individual's pursuit of his own interest contributes to the well-being of others. Thus, from the pursuit of individual interest, society is led, by an invisible hand, to the common good.

Smith showed that "self-interest" in the course of history had led to the specialization and division of labour. The exchange—through trade in markets—which naturally followed specialization, was responsible for the world's progress. As such it should be allowed to progress unhindered by government intervention.

2. COMPETITION

The achievement of community welfare through the pursuit of individual interest presumes a freely competitive market. Competition is rivalry among producers and consumers, bidding against one another for goods or sales. It is only through competition that more producers enter a market when profits are high, increasing supply and reducing the price. As such, the economic society envisaged by Smith was to be devoid of economic privileges, which hinder competition.

Competition has been criticized as being chaotic, but it is in fact an orderly process, a spontaneous rather than planned order that follows ethical rules, namely that of not harming others. Far from being destructive, rivalrous firms competing for scarce resources determine the best use of the resources by their bidding for them. Without this competition, we could not perform economic calculations, because in a complex economy there would be no way of knowing the relative scarcity of resources relative to consumer demand.

If competition is prevented from operating in any way, whether by organised groups, criminals, or legislation, the result is usually higher prices or a lower quality of goods and services, as well as the social waste of inefficiency.

Competition tends to eliminate profits other than normal returns to the factors of production. The firms that maintain the lowest costs of production will earn a greater share of profits. In an effort to keep costs of production down to a minimum every avenue of innovation will be explored. Indeed, the process of competition is essential to efficiency—it provides for cost saving innovations and induces firms to adapt to change.

One obvious barrier to competition is tariffs and quotas imposed at national borders. Another barrier is a governmental monopoly such as the postal service, or the domination of a service such as education by making the governmental service gratis, while those who prefer private services have to pay the price. Licenses are another barrier; they restrict entry into an industry to certain specified persons. The alleged reason is to assure some standard of competency, but the result is often restricted entry even for qualified practitioners.

3. MARKET STRUCTURE

The market structure of an industry consists of the number of firms and their relative size. Different market structures induce different types of outcomes. Economics categorizes four basic types of market structure.

atomistic competition

In economics there are two different meanings of "competition." One is rivalry, in which a greater share for one implies less for others. The second meaning of competition is "the degree of absence of pricing power." Pricing power is the ability to set a price. This is also referred to as market power. When economists refer to competition in market structure, they usually mean the second type, the relative absence of pricing power.

The most competitive structure, the one with the least pricing power, is the structure in which there are many, thousands and millions, of firms, none of which is large enough to affect the price of the product, and in which there are no barriers to the entry and exit of firms into that industry. This structure is called "atomistic" competition. For analysis, the hypothetical extreme case of an infinite number of firms and costless entry is called "perfect" competition, meaning a complete absence of pricing power. Many products in atomistic competition have basically the same outcome as with perfect competition.

In atomistic competition, a firm is so small relative to the rest of the industry that it must sell its output at the price set by industry supply and demand. The product is homogenous or uniform, so that if one firm tried to sell at a price a bit above the market, no one would buy it, since others are selling the same stuff for less. The firms are price takers, selling at the market price.

If firms in atomistic competition make economic profits (as discussed in Chapter 7), then new firms will enter the industry to obtain some profits. As the industry expands, the industry supply curve shifts out and hence price will be driven down the demand curve. Economic profits are therefore a short-run situation; in atomistic competition, the long-run equilibrium economic profit is zero, and the firms only make normal accounting profits that provide normal returns to the factors of production.

But what if one farm has superior land. Wheat farming may be an industry with atomistic competition, but would not the farms with better land will have more profit? They will have lower average costs, but the better land has a higher rent, so after subtracting out the rent from the accounting profit, the net economic profit is still zero. The "producer surplus" goes to rent.

But wait a minute! Each firm in atomistic competition has no control over the price, yet the industry price can move up and down as industry supply and demand curves shift. So how can industry prices change if no firm can change the price?

Here's how it works. Suppose we have a million wheat farmers. One farmer wants to sell his wheat. He calls a wholesale dealer. The wholesale dealer might be overstocked with wheat, so he calls his broker at the commodity exchange, where the wholesaler can buy or sell all he wants at the quoted price. In the commodity market, such as the Chicago Board of Trade, there are thousands of buy and sell bids being entered every minute. The price is set second-by-second by the brokers who match the bids to buy and offers to sell. No single bidder can dictate a price, but each bidder has a small influence by increasing the bid in one or the other direction. So the price is set in the commodity exchanges, where the broker adjusts the price to match buys and sells. The same concept applies in financial markets for stocks and bonds.

In atomistic competition, firms produce at the lowest possible cost, which is the industry's minimum average cost. Since profit is maximized at the quantity where marginal revenue equals marginal cost, and marginal revenue equals price, the price equals the marginal cost. This price is socially efficient, because the price, being on the demand curve, reflects the marginal willingness to buy. So the marginal willingness to buy equals the marginal cost, and we cannot get more efficient than that. If price is greater than marginal cost, we are better off producing the next unit. If marginal cost is greater than price, the next unit has a loss. So when price equals marginal cost, we are in economic heaven for that good.

monopoly

The other extreme of market structure is monopoly. A monopoly exists either when there is only a single seller of a particular good or service, or as a different type of monopoly, when there is no entry into the industry for the expansion of product. We can call the first type a number-monopoly or absolute monopoly, and the second an entry-monopoly. Economists today usually mean absolute monopoly when they use the term "monopoly," although classical economists also referred to entry-monopoly.

If there is only one firm in an industry, the firm's demand curve is that of the industry, so it has the ability to set either the price or quantity of output. Note that in a market economically it cannot do both, since if it sets a price, market demand will determine the output sold at that price. A government monopoly, operating outside a market, can of course dictate both price and quantity, forcing people to consume and pay a price.

A profit-maximizing absolute monopoly will set its price at the level where its marginal cost equals its marginal revenue. Since its demand curve slopes down, its marginal revenue curve slopes down too, and even steeper. This is because each extra unit of output is not only sold at a lower price, but all previous units are also sold at that lower price. The quantity that maximizes profit is that for which the marginal cost and marginal revenue curves intersect. At that quantity, the monopoly price is the point on the demand curve. The price minus the average total cost at that quantity is the economic profit.

Thus the monopoly can limit the quantity to maintain a higher price than would prevail in a competitive industry. Unless there are offsetting benefits, this reduction in quantity creates a loss to society, called a "deadweight loss."

A monopoly can also practice price discrimination, the practice of charging different prices to different types of users. Firms price discriminate when they have discounts to older people or children. In Eastern Europe, some hotels and expensive restaurants charge a higher price to tourists than to the locals. Price discrimination increases sales by adjusting the price to the elasticity of demand, with the demand of wealthier customers more inelastic, or less responsive to price increases, i.e. they continue to buy even at the higher price. Price discrimination both increases the profit and decreases the deadweight loss, since the firm can sell more at lower prices.

A monopoly having no current competition may face potential competition if its economic profits are consistently high, so it may be induced to keep its price below the short-run profit-maximizing level.

In entry-monopoly, even where there are many firms, they can earn economic profits, since other firms cannot enter to expand the output. An example of entry monopoly is taxi cabs in New York City; one needs a government permit to enter the field, but the number of permits is fixed, so to enter, one needs to buy a permit from a previous owner. Land, being fixed in supply, works the same way.

Types of absolute monopoly include locational monopoly, natural monopoly, new-product monopoly, and government-protected monopoly.

A locational monopoly is the only firm in some immediate market area, such as the only drug store in a small town. Such firms can have monopolistic profits, but these profits are limited by competition from farther-away firms and from the personal relationships that may develop in a small town.

A new-product monopoly is a temporary restriction against competition for creators of new literature (copyrights) and for new inventions (patents). A government-protected monopoly is a legal barrier to entry not warranted by new products.

Patents are a controversial form of monopoly. Some argue that patents are necessary to protect the investment in research of the inventor and stimulate new inventions; others that they give the inventor too much of a monopolistic privilege. Those who favor patents argue that they are a method of economizing on contracts. It would be costly for the maker of a new firm to make a contract with each buyer not to copy the item, especially to enforce such a contract. Patents, like copyrights, simplify the contract with a notice on the product that it is patented and a conventional number of years that the contract applies for. Patents also enable the inventor to register his invention and check to see that it is really new.

New-product monopolies may charge higher prices than they would in a competitive market structure, but these new products might not be brought to market otherwise, so the net result can be beneficial. This is not so for government-protected monopolies. Here, the public might pay a higher price and gets less output for no good economic reason.

A naturally monopoly occurs when there are economies of large scale. There is a large fixed cost and a small marginal cost, and it is not profitable for other firms to enter. Examples include municipal utilities such as piped water; a second firm would duplicate the pipes of the first, and bringing in water by truck is much more expensive.

One way government has dealt with natural monopolies is to set a price, usually at the average cost (including a normal accounting profit). A problem with this method is that the firm has little incentive to control costs, other than from government oversight and hearings, which may not be effective in controlling costs. The commissioners regulating a monopoly may have come from that industry and may in fact be working to benefit its owners rather than the public.

In many cases, the government runs the industry directly. In some cases, government enterprises such as trains and subways provide good service, though often not, but it is again difficult to control the costs, and the incentive of workers, often in a union, may be to increase their own benefits and power, which increases costs.

A third option is to periodically open control of the natural monopoly to a competitive bid. The industry itself is a monopoly, but bidding to own it for a while can be highly competitive. The highest bidder then runs the outfit for a certain period of time, charging what it pleases. But the government keeps the fee paid by the bidder. If the bidding is competitive, this fee represents the monopoly profit, which is now paid to the government. The company then has the incentive to minimize costs during its operations. This option is also not perfect, because the firm still charges the public a monopoly price, but it avoids the social waste of artificially high costs that may compensate for that.

A fourth option exists when the firm cannot make a profit only from the user charges, and the service is a territorial collective good that increases land rent. Suppose there is a subway in a city, which is a natural monopoly. Even maximizing profits, the revenues would not cover the costs. But there is a second profit in the increased land value and rent, which when added to the fares would make the operation profitable. The service can therefore be funded by a combination of rent and user charges, especially when the charges are based on the congestion of the service, charging more when it is crowded to compensate society for the crowding the users impose and to even out the usage.

Monopolistic Competition

Whereas with atomistic competition, there is a uniform product, with monopolistic competition, there are many firms, but there is product differentiation: each firm produces a different version of the product, such as a different style, brand, or location. Each firm also has a mild monopoly on its variant, the products being close substitutes. There are also no barriers to the entry of new firms and increased production. An examples of product differentiation is book publishing. There are hundreds of publishers producing similar books.

Because of this mild monopoly, each firm faces a downward-sloping demand curve, and has some control over price. These firms will then set prices where marginal costs equal marginal revenues. But over the long run, because of competition, there will tend to be no economic profits, firms operating where the price equals the average cost. But since this cost curve is tangent to the demand curve (coming down to touch it and then bouncing off), the firms are not operating at the minimum possible average cost.

Although the price is above marginal cost, and above minimum cost, product variety is valued by many people. Firms compete by advertising, which is not wasteful, since ads provide some information, and ads can act as a signal that the company has a quality product, otherwise it would not have repeat sales. Advertising also pays for newspapers, magazines, radio, television, and web sites.

It is unrealistic to expect markets where products are or can be differentiated to behave like those where they are uniform. The market has in fact produced generic brands as well that have less fancy labels for lower prices. Firms try to influence consumers, but in the end, consumers choices are voluntary. There is nothing imperfect about an outcome that is the best one can have given the conditions of the products.

Oligopoly

An oligopoly, an industry with few sellers, includes firms with a homogenous product such as oil and with a product differentiation such as cars.. There are often few firms in an industry due to economies of scale, which induce firms to become large. A firm in an oligopoly is very much affected by the action of any of its competitors, but exactly how it responds depends on circumstances. A type of game can be played by one firm lowering price and the others responding, and like chess, the oligopoly game has no one exact sequence of plays.

Oligopolists can collude to create an industry monopoly among them, either secretly or openly as a cartel. But there will be a great temptation to cheat on the agreement, since a firm that lowers its price just a bit will be able to sell much more product. If one or more of the firms sell below the cartel price, then eventually that price cannot be maintained, and the oligopoly will fall apart. Also, new firms may enter the industry to take advantage of the cartel price, and as the supply curve shifts outward, the increased product must be sold at a lower price. The cartel must either lower its price or fall apart. There can be an equilibrium in which no firm has any gain in reducing its price, each firm maximizing profits given the market shares of the others; this is referred to as a "Nash equilibrium," after the mathematician John Nash.

An economic "game" consists of interaction among players, rules, and payoffs for each player. A game can be cooperative or rival. Game outcomes can be positive sum, negative sum, or zero sum. A game can be one-time or repeated.

Game theory explains decision making with incomplete information. It involves strategies. "Strategic" means each player takes into account the likely reactions of other players.

A dominant strategy is one that is the best for a player, regardless of the actions of the others.

The most famous game is called the prisoners' dilemma. The story is that there are two thieves who get caught. They are partners in crime, but they don't care about each other. They are questioned in separate rooms. If one confesses and the other does not, the confessor goes free and the other 20 years in prison. If they both confess they get 8 years. If neither confesses, they get a lesser charge, and only 1 year in prison. The incentive is for both to confess. Confessing is the dominant strategy, even though they would both have been best off not confessing.

4. GOVERNMENT AND COMPETITION

The degree of oligopoly or industry concentration can be measured using the Herfindahl index. You first calculate the fraction of the industry that each firm has. Then square each fraction. Finally, add up the squares. The result is a concentration index between zero and one, one being a monopoly and a number close to zero being atomistic.

Governments have reacted to oligopolies and collusion with "anti-trust laws," breaking large firms (formerly called "trusts") into small ones. But the success of this policy has been questioned, since large firm size or high concentration does not necessarily imply that the market can be improved by intervention. Some firms become large because they provide superior goods and services—breaking them up would punish market success. Large firms can also capture the benefits of research, and focusing only on industry within a country overlooks the fact that we live in a global economy, and in a market economy, there can be plenty of rivalrous competition. Moreover, government agents do not have the knowledge needed to know just how much competition is optimal, and they are unable to know the unintended consequences of meddling in the market.

While trying to break up some industry oligopolies, governments sometimes deliberately create them with price controls and restrictions on entry. For example, some city governments limit the number of taxi cab firms and cars. Before 1978, the airline industry in the U.S. was prevented from competing in prices, and the entry of new firms was restricted. The industry therefore engaged in non-price competition, such as offering more luxurious service or more frequent flights on half-empty airplanes. Many consumers prefer lower prices to such high-cost services.

As noted, competition is not just the existence of many firms, but of rivalry among them. In a free market, rivalry for the consumer's marginal dollar or pound will ultimately win out against inefficiencies, since in a global economy any excess profits or costs are like bait to the hungry wolves stalking the woods for profit opportunities. The best that government can normally do is to take down the barriers but prevent the consumer sheep from being fleeced, with stiff laws against fraud, and easy access to the courts, making the loser of a lawsuit pay all legal costs.

Though competition is rivalrous, at the same time, firms have an incentive to cooperate where their interests are mutual. Firms create industry associations to provide them with research, information, and cameraderie. Hence, competition and cooperation are complements rather than opposites in a market economy. It is difficult enough to provide a sound legal basis for market processes without trying to improve outcomes when the cure may well be worse than the alleged disease.

The next chapter will take a closer look at the outcomes of our current economies and analyze them to see whether it is indeed the market or intervention that is the foundational cause.

Chapter 9: Social Problems

1. INEQUALITY

All large economies have unequal distributions of income. We first examine how to measure inequality, and then inquire as to why it is ubiquitous, existing in all cultures and economic systems, and the morality of equality.

A simplistic way to measure inequality is to count the percentage of the people with the top or bottom x% of income, such as saying that the top 10% own 50%. But to really measure the extent of inequality, we need to take account of the entire distribution, not just one part of it.

One widely-known way to depict inequality is the "Lorenz curve." This is a square with a diagonal drawn from the bottom left to the top right. The horizontal axis measures the cumulative percentage of population, with zero at the left and 100% at the right corners of the square, from the poorest (on the left) to the richest. For example, the point 3/4 of the way from the left indicates the lowest 75% of the population. The vertical axis plots the phenomenon being measured, such as income or wealth, with zero at the bottom and 100% at the top. If the distribution has complete equality, the Lorenz curve coincides with the diagonal line. The more unequal the distribution, the closer the curve to the bottom and right sides of the square. A totally unequal distribution would have one person owning everything and the rest nothing, which would be a curve along the bottom and right sides of the square.

The Lorenz curve can be used to generate a number that measures inequality, called the "Gini coefficient." This is calculated by measuring the area between the diagonal line and the Lorenz curve, and dividing it by the area of the triangle formed by the diagonal and the sides of the square. The greater the ratio, the greater the inequality. The Gini coefficient (G) can also be measured directly from the distribution. Let n be the number of persons or units in the distribution, y be the average income or wealth of the distribution, and y1 be the highest income (or wealth), y2 the second highest, etc., then G = 1 + 1/n - (2/(n2 * y)) * (y1 + 2 y2 + ... + nyn).

An easier way to calculate inequality is the "inequality index" developed by the author. First we measure the concentration of the distribution. Suppose the distribution is (50, 30, 20) for three persons. The Herfindahl concentration index is calculated by first computing the fraction of the total held by each person. This would be: (5/10, 3/10, 2/10). Then square each fraction: (25/100, 9/100, 4/100). Finally, add up the squares: the total in this case is (25+9+4)/100 = 38/100, or .38. This is the concentration index C. To get the inequality index I, simply multiply C by N: .38 * 3 = 1.14. Perfect equality has an index of 1, so the greater the inequality, the greater the index. For example, for three persons, if one had all and the other two had nothing, the index I equals 3.

To understand why inequalities exist, we can divide incomes by the returns to factors, as wages, rent, and capital yields (along with interest income, which originates in any of the three factors). Obviously, if the ownership of land and capital goods is unequal, then this explains a major source of income inequality. But then we can go deeper and inquire as to why assets are unequally owned.

Property is obtained by two methods: voluntarily and by force. Some wealth and a great amount of land has been obtained through conquest, which accounts for many great fortunes, and thus much inequality in places such as Latin America, where estates date back to the Spanish conquest. In some cases, monopoly power has been a source of income which is inherently unequal, and government-provided privileges and subsidies have been a key source of unequal income.

But a great deal of wealth has also been accumulated through voluntary means, by entrepreneurs and their lucky heirs. The profits of entrepreneurs are a return to their labor. Wages are unequal due to differing abilities, education, goals, effort, and just plain luck. Discrimination is also a cause of inequality, although in a prosperous market, it is a minor cause, since there are ample opportunities, including self-employment, and the market penalizes discrimination with higher costs and lower profits. Normally, effort plus talent are get their just rewards in a pure market economy. But when interventions create unemployment, employers can be more choosy, and are then able to discriminate against those they dislike.

Some social scientists have argued against income inequality, saying that a poor person values an extra dollar more than a rich person. But this is not universally so, and such subjective values cannot be measured or compared. Even if this is true for most people, it does not morally justify stealing wealth from the rich, and taxing the rich to benefit the poor would also create disincentives to create wealth, leading to less production and employment.

A sounder argument against inequality is that the rich can give their children a better head start, with better education and other opportunities. In a pure market economy, however, all have an opportunity to obtain an education and employ their labor, even though the wealthy have better opportunities. But again, the universal ethic does not permit stealing out of envy, and economically, such theft would reduce opportunities by reducing enterprise.

Much of the inequality that exists in the world today is not due to better talent or luck, but from privileges and plunder gained through government coercion, especially the taking of land from previous inhabitants. Taxes on wages deepen this cause by reducing the ability of workers to save income and accumulate capital.

As Henry George (1883, p. 9) stated, "at the bottom of every social problem we will find a social wrong." When the benefits of land and other natural resources are shared equally, a major cause of inequality is eliminated without resort to the forceful taking of legitimately earned wealth.

Taxes can be characterized by how they relate to inequality. A tax is called "progressive" if the tax rate is higher for higher amounts of the thing being taxed, whether income or property. A "regressive" tax has a higher rate for lower income or property. A flat or proportionate tax has the same rate for all levels of income or property. An income tax may appear to be progressive, with higher rates on higher incomes, but actually not be if high-income earners are able to avoid the tax with deductions and exemptions. Also, a tax or fee may appear to be proportionate, but actually be progressive. For example, if an assessment is paid by land owners, equal to the amount of their land rent, then the tax rate is proportional, with the same rate for all sites, but if the ownership of land is concentrated among the wealthy, then in effect the assessment is progressive.

Taxes are often imposed not just to raise revenue, but to redistribute income to something allegedly more just. But as Henry George (1883, p. 83) noted, "As to what is the just distribution of wealth there can be no dispute. It is that which gives wealth to him who makes it, and secures wealth to him who saves it." A just distribution is the outcome of a just process. And the universal ethic (described in Chapter 1) prescribes that the just process in the distribution of income is the full retention of wages and capital yields by those who produce wealth, and the sharing of the yield of land by members of a community. Whatever inequalities arise from this process stems ultimately from unequal talent, effort, and luck. Those inheriting past wealth, or talent, or finding luck, may not deserve them more than others, but justice is not about fairness in the fortunes of fate but the deeper equality of each person being able to freely pursue one's own life.

2. POVERTY: THE GREAT ENIGMA OF ECONOMICS

We began this book with the question of prosperity and social justice, and the realization that our ideals must be founded on sound principles. The first eight chapters have laid out the principles of micro-economics, the theoretical foundation of economics. We will now apply them to analyze the issues of poverty, economic inequality, unemployment, and other social problems.

The greatest problem in economics is the explanation for and solution of poverty. The French economists of the 1700s, whose school of thought is called "Physiocracy" (the rule of natural law), examined the poverty of French peasantry and proposed free trade and a tax only on "net product," which we now recognize as rent. Adam Smith also called for unrestricted, free exchange as the way to create the "wealth of nations." David Ricardo analyzed free trade further and also noted the suitability of land as a source of revenue. Henry George, therefore, did not really break new ground in his policy that called for free trade and a tax only on land rent, but he was foremost in focusing on the problem of poverty in the midst of progress, on just why advancing wealth and technology did not eradicate poverty.

George starts his classic *Progress and Poverty* with a statement of the puzzle:

"At the beginning of this marvelous era it was natural to expect, and it was expected, that laborsaving inventions would lighten the toil and improve the condition of the laborer; that the enormous increase in the power of producing wealth would make real poverty a thing of the past" (p. 3). Not only could one expect material prosperity for all, but also, in lifting everyone from want and economic anxiety, the moral uplifting of social life:

"And out of these bounteous material conditions he would have seen arising, as necessary sequences, moral conditions realizing the golden age of which mankind have always dreamed.

Youth no longer stunted and starved; age no longer harried by avarice ... discord turned into harmony!" (pp. 4–5). This is not to say we would have utopia, but that the core of our economic problems would disappear, making other social problems, such as raising our children as sympathetic members of society, much easier to resolve.

Such were the hopes of enlightened people at the dawn of the industrial age. George wrote 100 years after the beginning of the industrial revolution, and it is now another 100 years later. The idea of progress has remained popular, but, as George wrote, "Now, however, we are coming into collision with facts which there can be no mistaking. From all parts of the civilized world come complaints of industrial depression; of labor condemned to involuntary idleness; of capital massed and wasting; of pecuniary distress among businessmen; of want and suffering and anxiety among the working classes" (pp. 5–6).

That these words apply today just as much as they did 100 years ago is a sad testimony to the failure of our institutions to have implemented the remedies for these problems. This in part is due to the economic ignorance of the public, which is exploited by authorities. Armed with economic knowledge, the public will demand that the remedies be applied immediately and no longer be fooled by fallacies and economic quackery.

For George then points out that the existence of similar problems throughout the world cannot come from local and unique causes. These problem occur under many cultures, historical settings, and types of government. "Evidently," he wrote, "beneath all such things as these, we must infer a common cause" (p. 6). Moreover, a study of new territories versus old ones and the history of economic development demonstrate that while people may start out in equality, as an economy develops, as wealth grows, so too does poverty. Social difficulties are "engendered by progress itself ... The promised land flies before us like the mirage" (p. 8).

George, of course, does not deny that on an absolute scale, the condition of many workers has improved with technical progress. But the lowest classes still lie in the muck of poverty—witness the homeless in the U.S.A. today, and the slums of the inner cities. "Those who are above the point of separation are elevated, but those who are below are crushed down" (p. 9). So, George poses the problem:

"This association of poverty with progress is the great enigma of our times. It is the central fact from which spring industrial, social, and political difficulties that perplex the world, and with which statesmanship and philanthropy and education grapple in vain. From it come the clouds that overhang the future of the most progressive and self-reliant nations. It is the riddle which the Sphinx of Fate puts to our civilization and which not to answer is to be destroyed. So long as all the increased wealth which modern progress brings goes but to build up great fortunes, to increase luxury and make sharper the contrast between the House of Have and the House of Want, progress is not real and cannot be permanent" (p. 10).

As George (1883, p. 81) stated, "For every social wrong there must be a remedy. But the remedy must be nothing less than the abolition of the social wrong."

But instead of eliminating the cause, many political interests have come forth with superficial treatments of the effects. Quack economic medicine can be recognized by noting that it only treats effects, ignoring the causes. Even eminent economists such as J. M. Keynes have misdiagnozed the cause as inherent instability in markets, requiring government intervention, when in fact it is interference in the natural economy that has caused the turbulence in the first place. Quack remedies include the ideas that "labor and capital" are in fundamental conflict, that automation and technical progress is responsible for unemployment, that profits or interest are evils, that more and more money can solve a "lack of demand," and that the government has to pump up investment and demand. Such ideas, recognized George, bring the masses under the power of "charlatans and demagogues" (p. 11).

But economics can tell us the answer, by examining the causes and their consequences. This we have done. We have the philosophical foundation in Chapter 1 and the three resources or factors of production in Chapters 2 through 4. There we saw that the margin of production determines the wage level, and that the wealth produced after the payment of wages and the return to capital constitutes rent. We saw how as the margin extends to poorer lands, wages decrease while rent increases, and how rent also vastly increases as communities and commerce arises. We saw how land speculation accelerates these trends by using up land faster than warranted by current use, decreasing wages by moving the margin of production to less productive land. We saw how the use of more capital goods increases wages, but increases rent also, and how wages declined back again if the capital goods extend the margin once again to less productive lands. Competition can lead to efficient production, but cannot by itself raise wages which have been driven down to an unproductive margin.

We have seen also how the taxation of wages makes workers poorer and reduces employment, while the taxation of production, trade, and enterprise reduces the amount of production from what would otherwise take place, reducing employment and wealth. Workers at the bottom, or those without work, and thus squeezed in the double pincers of costs imposed by government and, over the long run, ever-increasing rent. The diversion of the rent to the holders of land title is not a part of a pure market, since much intervention consists of taxing labor to provide public works that benefit especially the owners of land, thus transferring income from workers to landowners.

But government restrictions and costs are imposed, in part to treat the effects of social problems, in part due to special interests that lobby and pressure for privileged benefits with the excuse of benefiting the public, and in part due to ignorance about the causes and effects. Social problems thus provide manure for ever more taxes and restrictions. Hence, the original and ultimate cause is as described by George (p. 282): "The reason why, in spite of the increase of productive power, wages constantly tend to a minimum which will give but a bare living [for those at the lowest end of the wage scale], is that, with increase in productive power, rent tends to even greater increase, thus producing a constant tendency to the forcing down of wages."

"As land increases in value, poverty deepens and pauperism appears. In the new settlements, where land is cheap, you will find no beggars, and the inequalities in condition are very slight. In the great cities, where land is so valuable that it is measured by the foot, you will find the extremes of poverty and of luxury" (p. 288).

Suppose a great island arose in the ocean, on which people could cultivate plants that would give them twice the wage in the old country. What would happen to wages in the old country. As workers leave the old country, rent rapidly decreases as marginal land is abandoned for the new land, and thus wages rapidly rise. With good free land available, rents in the old country must fall and wages must rise.

Now imagine, as George did (p. 294) that a small village grows into a large city. Will wages be higher, will the return on capital be greater? No. What, then, will be higher? "Rent; the value of land. Go, get yourself a piece of ground, and hold possession." And when the city is built, we will find luxurious mansions armed with guards and alarms to protect themselves from the thieves and muggers that fester in the slums.

Though poverty in the midst of progress has puzzled even economists who should know better, "so simple and clear is this truth, that to see it fully once is always to recognize it" (p. 295). George describes those pictures made up of a labyrinth of lines, which you can keep staring at but can't make out—"until once the attention is called to the fact that these things make up a face or a figure." One follower of George looked at just such a picture, and then realized it showed a cat. Once he saw the cat, the figure was clear and obvious. Adherents of George's thought henceforth have said that when one grasps the central idea of the cause of poverty, you have "seen the cat!" The jumble of economic activity become clear, as springing from a central principle: "The great cause of inequality in the distribution of wealth is inequality in the ownership of land." Land has been the foundation of great fortunes, as said the Brahmins ages ago (George, p. 296):

"To whomsoever the soil at any time belongs, to him belong the fruits of it. White parasols and elephants mad with pride are the flowers of a grant of land."

Governments throughout the world react to poverty mostly by treating the symptoms rather than the underlying causes. Old-age insurance, medical aid, food coupons, government housing, and welfare payments may prevent the poor from suffering, but they do not cure the problem. They instead perpetuate poverty, first by funding these programs with taxes on production, reducing employment and wages, and secondly, by making it costly for the poor to escape poverty, since they both lose benefits and get taxed if they obtain employment. Minimum wages compound the problem by preventing the least able from working legally. Laws prohibiting drugs create large profit opportunities to those in the slums but the resulting violence and crime makes it even less desirable for business to employ people there.

Only a policy that removes the cause of poverty will cure it permanently. The ultimate antipoverty program is the desire of each person to better his or her own condition. All that is really needed is to avoid putting barriers in the way of self-improvement.

George (1883, p. 78) put the matter very succinctly: "There is in nature no reason for poverty." Remove the restrictions and tax barriers to employment and collect revenue from site rents instead. The elimination of taxation will raise the wage at the margin, and the collection of the land rent will, by eliminating the speculative and consumptive ownership of less productively used land, move the margin toward more productive land. With this remedy, the poverty problem will rapidly melt away as communities regenerate themselves spontaneously.

3. UNEMPLOYMENT

A person is "unemployed" if she or he is willing and able to work at the prevailing wage rate, but is unable to find employment. As George (1879, p. 5) put it, the unemployed are "condemned to involuntary idleness." Since an alternative to being employed by others is to become self-employed, the presence of unemployment implies also that it is difficult or infeasible to start one's own enterprise as well.

But why should this be? George (1879, p. 270) called it a "strange and unnatural spectacle" that willing workers "cannot find employment." In his book Social Problems (p. 8), George illustrates how odd this really is:

"Give us but a market," say manufacturers, "and we will supply goods without end." "Give us but work!" cry idle men.

Is it possible that the number of jobs might be limited? But people can create their own jobs, so this must imply that all desires have been filled. But the 10th foundational proposition of economics, as stated in Chapter 1, states that human desires tend to be unlimited. There cannot be too much production in general, especially so when "people suffer for the lack of things that labor produces" (George, 1879, p. 270). Hence, there is always a demand for labor to fulfill these desires. The other original factor of production being land, labor can always be applied to land, unless something is blocking it—"somewhere there is an obstacle which prevents labor from producing the things that laborers want" (p. 271).

One possible block is a shortage of land, of natural resources. If the economy an area of the earth, such as a desert, is mainly geared to using the scanty vegetation, such as for grazing, then too many users will lead to poverty, but not necessarily to unemployment, unless the land is closed off to additional users. Here, then, is the key to unemployment. The problem is not an overall lack of natural resources. If that were so, the prices of basic commodities such as metals and grains would be going up as they became scarcer. But this has not happened. Even with today's massive population, the earth has plenty of resources available. We are not running out of oil, metals, agricultural land, or living space.

Some unemployment is short term and an unavoidable part of a dynamic economy in which enterprises change and workers search for better opportunities. This "frictional" unemployment consists of the time needed for job search, such as getting information and interviewing. This "natural unemployment" is not part of the jobless problem.

Another type of unemployment is called "structural." As some industries shrink or move to better locations, workers are left stranded. To be employed at their accustomed wages, they need to move or to become retrained. Again, this is natural in a dynamic economy, and in a free market, the prospering industries can absorb this structural unemployment, which again is temporary. "Full employment" is thus defined not as 100% employment, which is not even desirable, but as the situation in which the only unemployment is short-term frictional or structural.

"Cyclical" unemployment occurs during the depression phase of a business cycle, when many workers are laid off and can't easily find work because the entire economy is depressed. The remedy is to eliminate such cycles, as is discussed in the chapter on business cycles.

The unemployment problem as such is not the frictional, structural, or even cyclical types (which is primarily a cycle problem), but the chronic joblessness in which workers cannot find jobs even during more prosperous times, and often remain unemployed for years. Why would labor be continuously unemployed?

If the problem is not a lack of land, or natural resources, it must be that some barriers have been erected between land and labor. Something is blocking the ability of labor to freely access natural resources to produce wealth. Who has done this? The only institution with the power to prevent labor from mixing with land is government.

The barriers erected by government include the prohibitions, restrictions, and taxes imposed on labor and enterprise, as well as barriers indirectly caused by government policy. As discussed in Chapter 2 on labor, high taxes create a wedge between the cost of labor to an employer (including the self-employed) and the net earnings of an employee. By making labor more expensive, this tax wedge reduces employment. Taxes on enterprise reduce profits and sales, and therefore reduce employment. Policy which induces land speculation (such as public works that increase land rent while not collecting that rent to finance the works) can raise the price of land above that warranted by present uses, thus reducing current enterprise and employment.

The situation becomes even worse when restrictions are imposed, such as minimum wage laws. Labor that would have been employed at the below-minimum rate now is unemployable. Unemployment insurance and welfare enable the unemployed to eat, but make it even more difficult to find employment, since switching from welfare to employment typically brings little extra reward for the lowest-paid workers.

Other restrictions, preventing people from working in certain occupations, days and hours, and other costs, such as the costs of filling out forms and making it difficult to fire workers, result in even less demand for labor and the attempt to substitute machinery for workers.

Employment is like a race around a track. If we put up high hurtles that the runners must leap over, the most able and determined can jump them, but the others cannot. The least able and motivated become unemployed. But if we remove all the hurtles, then all runners can go through, even the weak ones. Let the walls come tumbling down—eliminate the barriers of taxes and restrictions, and all willing and able to work shall be employed.

Unemployment is not only a personal and social tragedy, but wasteful of labor. As George (1883, p. 76) put it, "this enormous waste of productive power is due, not to defects in the laws of nature, but to social maladjustments which deny to labor access to the natural opportunities of labor and rob the laborer of his just reward."

Chapter 10: The Pure Market Economy

1. THE COLLECTION OF LAND RENT

If people are free to conduct their economic lives as they please, so long as they do not coercively harm others, in accord with the universal ethic described in Chapter 1, then they live in a free society with a free market. The ideal market economy is built on a legal foundation in which human rights, including property rights, are protected. Its two main principles are 1) self ownership—each person owns his or her life and labor, and 2) paying rent for the possession and use of natural resources, since land cannot be claimed from self-ownership.

Economic land rent is the potential, if not actual, yield on land exclusive of the capital goods tied to land, such as buildings. The amount of rent is determined by the value of the uses to which the land can be applied. Some rental value is due to natural features, such as sunlight and rain for farm land. For urban land, the bulk of value is due to human action: population and commerce create a demand to be located in this territory, increasing rent and land value. Still more site value and rentals are created by civic goods and services, such as transportation, security, and parks. This rental generated by civic goods can collected by the agency providing the goods, which can include private proprietary communities and residential associations as well as governments.

But will rent alone supply enough revenue for government? Several studies have found rent to amount to between a fifth and a third of national income (Foldvary, 2006). Land rent comes from three basic sources: 1) natural benefits, such as proximity to water; 2) population and commerce; 3) civic works. On the third source, the increase in rent generated by civic services determines the socially desirable amount of the service. If a service does not generate enough rent to cover the cost, then it should not be provided. On the other hand, there is no such market measuring device for taxes on labor, interest, wealth, profits, and value added. Moreover, since economic land includes all space, including the seas and the atmosphere, fees for pollution are in effect rent paid for dumping on that land, which when added to the rent of surface sites more than adequately covers public expenditures. Given a certain budgeted amount of spending B, and an amount of funds raised from other rents and user fees R, the amount charged for pollution can be B - R.

If industries are to take full advantage of the economies of scale which exist within cities, the revenue from land rent must be used to supplement the fees charged by these decreasing cost activities, such as busses and subways. This is not a subsidy, since the transportation, street, park, etc., induces that very rent that is then used to finance it.

The reason lies in the important distinction between marginal and average cost pricing. Marginal cost is the increase in costs due to the expansion of production by one unit. Average cost is the total cost of production divided by number of units. Since the marginal cost of an increasing-return (or decreasing-cost) industry is below its average cost, if its prices are set at the short-run marginal cost, the revenue will not cover the fixed costs of production.

Thus, revenue derived from land rents is efficiently used to supplement the revenues of decreasing-cost industries raised by pricing according to the marginal costs, to defray those fixed costs of services which are not marginally attributable to the amount of output. The funds from land rent are, however, only efficient if the service generates such rents in a free market.

An illustrative example would be the case of mass transit and other forms of transportation. If transportation is funded by land rent to cover its fixed costs, it can afford to price its output at levels which represent the marginal cost of supplying the service. In some cases, the provision of transportation is not even funded by marginal pricing at all, or else the marginal cost is free. Hotels, for example, do not charge for the use of the elevators, the cost being included in the room charges, which amounts to a type of rent. As demand increases, the producer can expand output, thereby allowing the service to take full advantage of its economy of scale. Finally, with lower prices and an expanded service more people would be encouraged to use mass transportation and thereby reduce the diseconomies of other modes of travel, such as congestion on the roads.

In a society which seeks to limit government involvement in the market place, subsidies would be shunned as producing waste and inefficiency. But if the funding is derived from the rent generated, then no subsidy is made. Projects which increase site rents transfer tax-payers' money into the land-owner's pocket. The provision of such public services financed by land rent conforms to the benefit principle of public finance, and is similar to the market provision of services, being neither an arbitrary cost nor a subsidy. Such services can be and have been provided by private organizations as well, along these very principles (see Foldvary, 1994).

2. THE OUTCOME OF A PURE MARKET ECONOMY

In a pure market economy, there are no restrictions or taxes on productive effort, including labor, enterprise, sales, and profits. Community services, whether provided by government or by private firms or associations, are funded by user fees and land rent, including charges for pollution. How would such a world differ from ours?

The claimed benefits of the community collection of rent (CCR), often under the rubric of land-value taxation, have been regarded as exaggerated. Not only have the proponents of CCR pointed out its efficiency and equity relative to taxation, but they have also claimed that it would greatly reduce if not eliminate unemployment and poverty, and with them many of our social problems such as crime, drug abuse, and urban sprawl.

Perhaps it will cure cancer too!

These benefits do not stem only from sharing rent, but from eliminating the barriers that now intervene between enterprise and resources. If CCR is a panacea, it is only because there is one universal anti-panacea, a universal cause of social distress—the use of force to prevent labor from freely accessing natural resources. Removing this barrier is like taking down a dam—the waters of enterprise will come gushing forth. We see this time and again when countries have liberalized their economies. Is it not interesting that when the rulers of socialist economies wish to perk up their economies a bit, they reduce, not increase, taxes and restrictions.

As Henry George (1879, p. 433) states, "With all the burdens removed which now oppress industry and hamper exchange, the production of wealth would go on with a rapidity now undreamed of." It would be, he said, "like removing an immense weight from a powerful spring.... The present method of taxation operates on exchange like artificial deserts and mountains; it costs more to get goods through a custom house than it does to carry them around the world" (p. 434). Government punishes people with taxes for building and producing as though they were crimes. It is the removal of burdens, of restrictions and taxes and other imposed costs, that would stimulate production, increase employment, and raise wages. Exactly how much, no one can know. But with over 90% of workers employed even with these burdens, it is reasonable to conclude that the remaining 10% would be in demand with the abolition of taxes on labor and enterprise. As evidence, we can see the prosperity of Hong Kong and the high wages in Switzerland, which have relatively more freedom than other countries, yet are also far from pure market economies.

As George put it (p. 461): "Give labor a free field and its full earnings; take for the benefit of the whole community that fund which the growth of the community creates, and want and the fear of want would be gone. The springs of production would be set free, and the enormous increase of wealth would give the poorest ample comfort. Men would no more worry about finding employment than they worry about finding air to breathe; they need have no more care about physical necessities than do the lilies of the field. The progress of science, the march of invention, the diffusion of knowledge, would bring their benefits to all." This progress has two benefits, the direct and indirect. We already benefit from the direct effect, from the knowledge itself, but the indirect effect is to raise land rent. With CCR, we would all equally benefit from this second effect as well, rather than it going to landowners who contributed nothing to the progress of technology.

Even if unemployment is not totally eliminated, eliminating much of it will also have positive social effects, just as high unemployment has negative effects, increasing crime, drug and alcohol abuse, and generally demoralizing communities. As George says, "Every productive enterprise, besides its return to those who undertake it, yields collateral advantages to others" (p. 435). These benefits are called "positive externalities" or "external effects." If you plant a tree, the whole neighborhood benefits from its beauty. And as George recognized, these territorial externalities increase rent: "And in the value or rent of land is this general gain expressed in a definite and concrete form."

As noted in Chapter 3, the community collection of rent reduces the selling price of land, the formula being $p = r/(i+c)$ where p is the price of land, i is the real interest rate, and c is the collection rate, the percentage of the land price p being collected. For example, if $c = .5$, then the annual assessment equals half the price of land. As c goes up, p must go down.

This decrease in selling price implies that enterprises do not have to borrow large sums of money to acquire land. The rental payment to the community takes the place of a mortgage. This frees up loan funds for paying for capital and labor. Interest rates would then drop, since there is much less demand for loans for real estate, and the decrease in interest rates stimulates enterprise even more. The elimination of land speculation also decreases the cost of land for both enterprise and home owners, and, combined with a sound banking system, would dampen if not eliminate the business cycle and depressions. Land being held for speculation would be put on the market for immediate use, and the more efficient use of land would again increase productivity and increase employment and wages. CCR would put in motion an upward spiral of ever increasing productivity and employment.

"Consider the effect of such a change upon the labor market. Competition would no longer be one-sided, as now. Instead of laborers competing with each other for employment, and in their competition cutting down wages to the point of bare subsistence, employers would everywhere be competing for laborers, and wages would rise to the fair earnings of labor. For into the labor market would have entered the greatest of all competitors for the employment of labor, a competitor whose demand cannot be satisfied until want is satisfied—the demand of labor itself. The employers of labor would not have merely to bid against other employers, all feeling the stimulus of greater trade and increased profits, but against the ability of laborers to become their own employers upon the natural opportunities freely opened to them … The spectacle of willing men unable to turn their labor into the things they are suffering for would become impossible."

Although the extent of these benefits cannot be forecast, the direction towards substantially reducing unemployment and poverty has a sound theoretical basis, and we need only compare those countries which have tried economic freedom even on a small scale—such as the growing East Asian economies—to those which have not, to see empirical verification of the benefits from freeing enterprise from imposed barriers and costs.

And these benefits also had advantages for the distribution of wealth. Much of the unequal ownership of wealth stems from a highly unequal ownership of land. The pattern typical in much of Latin America, for example, is for much of the farm land to be owned by a small number of wealthy families. But even in the United States, land ownership is highly concentrated, especially commercial land.

The collection of land rent by communities and governments, its benefit shared equally by the population, would eliminate one of the greatest causes of inequality, one which does nothing to further production. On the other hand, inequalities of wages due to different talent and effort would be left undisturbed, so that those with the greatest ability, education, and determination would have the full incentive to produce and create wealth.

As an economy grows, land rent tends to increase more than proportionately, so the equalization of the benefits of the rent equalizes the benefits from progress that spill over to a community as a whole.

Henry George recognized that the removal of barriers would stimulate technology as well. "It is mind, not muscle, which is the great agent of production" (p. 444). "The increase in the reward of labor and capital would still further stimulate invention and hasten the adoption of improved processes, and these would truly appear, what in themselves they really are—an unmixed good. The injurious effects of laborsaving machinery upon the working classes, that are now so often apparent, and that, in spite of all argument, make so many people regard machinery as an evil instead of a blessing, would disappear" (p. 445).

George, as a social philosopher as well as economist, recognized that CCR would have profound effects on social life beyond the advance of material welfare. "Noticeable among these is the great simplicity which would become possible in government. To collect taxes, to prevent and punish evasions, to check and countercheck revenues drawn from so many distinct sources," all these complications would be dispensed with (p. 454). CCR would also eliminate much of the transfer-seeking, the lobbying of government for favors, since first, there would ideally be constitutional measures preventing such privileges, and secondly, the absence of taxation would make this seeking more difficult politically. Because, as local officials know, few taxes get so much resistance to increases as a charge on real estate. Because CCR gets capitalized into lower property values, any extra government spending would imply funding from land rent, which would stir an opposition from landowners. And if CCR was a fixed amount, then this cap would also limit privilege-seeking.

The rise in wages that would flow from increased prosperity would reduce the economic causes of crime. The elimination of complex taxes and of much crime would then reduce "the great host of lawyers who are now [even in 1879!] maintained at the expense of producers; and talent now wasted in legal subtleties would be turned to higher pursuits" (p. 455).

While government as a repressive power would be reduced, governance as such would not be limited in a free society. People could join voluntary organizations, including civic and residential associations, which would provide whatever the members wished. Many of these would be territorial and collect the rents generated by their own services (see Foldvary, 1994). "Government would change its character, and would become the administrator of a great co-operative society" (p. 456).

In George's vision, social behavior would become transformed by universal prosperity. Human nature itself would not change, but the changed economic environment would induce the more benevolent aspect of human nature to become more dominant and the more greedy and apathetic aspects to become less so. Adam Smith in The Theory of Moral Sentiments (1790, p. 9) recognized that "How selfish soever man may be supposed, there are evidently some principles in his nature, which interest him in the fortune of others, and render their happiness necessary to him, though he derives nothing from it except the pleasure in seeing it."

These principles he called "sympathy" by which he meant "our fellow-feeling with any passion whatever" (p. 10). Sympathy is a feeling of affinity and empathy with another person, group, culture, or project. Henry George (1879, p. 458), in words similar to Smith, stated: "The desire for approbation, the feeling that urges us to win the respect, admiration, or sympathy of our fellows, is instinctive and universal."

George felt that greed need not be "the strongest of human motives" (1879, p. 457). Often, greed comes from poverty or the fear of not having enough in the future. When prosperity assures all who wish to work a well-paying wage, greed would be replaced by benevolence (p. 461): "With this abolition of want and the fear of want, the admiration of riches would decay, and men would seek the respect and approbation of their fellows in other modes than by the acquisition and display of wealth." George was perhaps too optimistic about the reduction in the desire for wealth, which is anyway not necessarily harmful to others. The more important point is that the prosperity assured by the pure market economy would reduce greed—the desire for undeserved gain - and promote sympathy with one's community and with fellow human beings. Economics alone would not do this, since upbringing and ethical education are also needed in order to instill sympathy among the population. But at least the economic incentives would be in the direction of benevolence.

Neo-classical economics is based almost entirely on the premise of self-interest. But to George (p. 462), "Shortsighted is the philosophy which counts on selfishness as the master motive of human action ... If you would move men to action, to what shall you appeal? Not to their pockets, but to their patriotism; not to selfishness, but to sympathy. Self-interest is, as it were, a mechanical force—potent, it is true; capable of large and wide results. But there is in human nature what may be likened to a chemical force; which melts and fuses and overwhelms; to which nothing seems impossible. 'All that a man hath will be give for his life' [Job 2:4] - that is self-interest. But in loyalty to higher impulses men will give even life."

Whereas in modern neo-classical thought, even when sympathy is acknowledged, self-interest is seen as the dominant motive, George (p. 463) thought the opposite: "Call it religion, patriotism, sympathy, the enthusiasm for humanity, or the love of God—give it what name you will; there is yet a force which overcomes and drives out selfishness; a force which is the electricity of the moral universe; a force beside which all others are weak ... And this force of forces ... we may use for the strengthening, and building up, and ennobling of society, if we but will, just as we now use physical forces that once seemed but powers of destruction. All we have to do is but to give it freedom and scope."

Though a society in which goodwill and benevolence are the norm seems utopian to some, George showed how circumstances can make it so in his example of a dinner party. In a company of "well-bred men and women dining together," where the food is plentiful, the people don't greedily grab food away from others. "On the contrary, each one is anxious to help his neighbor before he partakes of himself." Indeed, if anyone behaves greedily and disregards others, "the swift and heavy penalty of social contempt and ostracism would show how such conduct is reprobated by common opinion" (p. 464). George noted that this behavior is common at such parties, and if social conditions were like the party, with enough wealth for all to live adequately and equitably, with no fear of want, society would be like that too.

George adds that eliminating injustice and poverty would not destroy the "stimulus to exertion," because "desire would remain" (p. 466). "It is not labor in itself that is repugnant to man" (p. 467). Released from poverty and fear, people would work harder and better, motivated not so much by necessity but by the pride and satisfaction of producing, creating, and contributing. Great artists do not create for bread. Lesser artists too are motivated by more than groceries. As George said (p. 468), "the work which improves the condition of mankind ... is not done to secure a living ... It is the work of men who perform it for its own sake ... In a state of society where want was abolished, work of this sort would be enormously increased." People would be able, both in work and in leisure, to develop their minds—George recognized that many people have latent abilities that lie dormant due to lost opportunities (p. 469).

The elimination of restrictions and taxes on enterprise has a cascading effect, one benefit leading to another. Universal prosperity will have more than material consequences; it will improve the moral and social life of humanity. This does not imply that there will be a utopia. There would continue to be problems of personality conflicts and cultural clashes. Bias and negative attitudes are not so easily eliminated. But the gross economic problems and the social problems stemming from them would become history, just as chattel slavery has been eliminated from much of the earth. We cannot have utopia, but we can have a much better world, and the economic knowledge required to achieve it is known.

The question in achieving a new world of prosperity, justice, and harmony is: how do we deal with the ultimate problems blocking the way? The ultimate causes of social problems are *ignorance, apathy, and greed* (Foldvary, 1998). Education will overcome ignorance, movements for reform informed by proper education will overcome apathy, and then a sound economy and government will overcome greed.

Chapter 11: Money, Inflation, and Banking

1. THE ORIGIN AND NATURE OF MONEY

Money is a medium of exchange, which means that its function is to facilitate the exchange of goods. Without money, we would have a direct exchange of goods, or barter. Goods would exchange directly for other goods. With money, we have indirect exchange: you exchange a good for money (such as trading your labor for dollars), and then you exchange your money for other goods. The unique nature of money is that it is a good which can be easily exchanged for any other good. Money becomes the final means of payment; you can exchange goods for money substitutes such as IOU notes, but ultimately these notes are exchangeable for money.

A medium of exchange implies that it is also a "unit of account," which means it includes some measurement unit by which the value of all other goods can be measured. For example, if gold is used as money, the unit can be a gram or ounce. The value of goods is then calculated in terms of grams or ounces. In the U.S., the unit of account is the dollar, and in the U.K. it is the pound. These once referred to weights of gold, but now there are simply artificial units, accepted by law and custom.

Money originated in many societies for several reasons. First, with much trading, barter becomes inefficient, since you can't always find someone who wants your particular goods. Some commodities can be much more easily exchanged than others, and these become a medium of exchange. Shells, cacao beans, salt, cattle, gold, and silver have been such mediums, since they transported and measured more easily than other commodities. Gold and silver became widely used because of their high value, durability, and divisibility. A second origin of money was temple worship. Pieces of metal were used as offerings to deities. These became valued generally by the community and evolved into media of exchange. Gold and silver eventually became coined into pieces with standard shapes and weights.

The value of money relative to other goods today depends on its value yesterday. Though originating as a tradeable commodity, money takes on a life of its own, and its exchange value can become different from that of the original commodity, since the commodity gets extra value from being used as money. The relative value of the money units becomes established by custom, though it can evolve.

While originating in private and religious practice, governments took over the coining of money. In recent decades, money has become a government monopoly called "legal tender." Paper money originated as receipts for money stored with goldsmiths. During the 20th century, governments stopped the convertibility of paper notes into metals, and paper continued to circulate out of habit. Now the world uses "fiat money," which is valued only because the government mandates it.

Money is financial wealth, but not real or economic wealth. Real wealth consists of produced things, such as buildings, automobiles, and computers. If an earthquake destroys buildings, this is a real economic loss. But if all the money in a city were burned, there is little real loss. Since a $100 bill can be printed at a cost of one or two pennies, the money can be reprinted at low expense, and if we have a record of who held the money, we can give it all back and everything is back to normal!

If we double the amount of money in an economy and the amount of goods stays the same, generally their prices will double. So the amount of wealth has not doubled just because the amount of money is doubled, since the real wealth consists of the goods. The money claims simply lose half their exchange value for real wealth. We cannot arbitrarily increase the amount of wealth just by printing money, in contrast to real wealth, which is indeed increased when more is produced.

Therefore, money is not real wealth but a "claim" on wealth, just as a ticket to a show does not have value except that it can be exchanged for attendance at the show. We can burn the tickets and still let you into the show. Similarly, bonds are not real wealth, but a claim on wealth. If gold is used as money, however, it is real wealth, since melted gold has a market value as a commodity. But the real value of a gold coin is the melt value of the gold, which can be less than the exchange value of the coin.

When people deposit cash in a checking account in a bank, it is called a "demand deposit" because you can demand your money in cash at any time. Economists consider demand deposits to be money just like cash, since these funds are available for spending just by writing a check or using a debit card, both of which withdraw the money from your account. Savings accounts are considered a secondary type of money, and economists have various names for these, such as M1, M2, and so on. We will not be concerned with these distinctions here, which can be studied more thoroughly in a course on money and banking (and vary from country to country). We will, for simplicity, consider money to be cash and demand deposits.

The "demand for money" is the amount of money that people in an economy want to hold. People hold money for transactions (ordinary purchases) and for precaution, in case they need to buy something in a hurry. The "price level" is an index of prices relative to changes in the index at some other time. Mathematically, the price level is calculated by the formula: $P = MV/T$, where P is the price level, M is the total stock of money, V is the "velocity" or turnover of money, and T is the total amount of transactions measured by a price-level index of 1. For example, we can say that the prices as of January 1, 1995, will have a price level of 1, P at other times measured relative to that one.

Here is a simple example. Suppose on January 1, 1995, the economy has only two goods, bread and pens. Bread costs $1 per loaf, and a pen costs 50c. We set $P = 1$. The total amount of money M is $15.

During one year, we buy twenty pens and twenty loaves of bread, so T = 20*(1+.5) = 30. Since velocity V = PT/M, V is 1*30/15 = 2. The turnover of money is 2: each dollar is spent twice each year.

It is now January 1, 1996. The velocity of money is unchanged. The same amounts of both bread and pens are purchased per year, so T, measured in 1995 dollars, is still 30. But the money supply has doubled to $30. Then P = MV/T = 30*2/20 = 2. Prices have doubled. So if the turnover or velocity of money does not change and the total amount of production does not change, but the amount of money goes up, the price level will also go up. That's called "inflation."

2. INFLATION AND DEFLATION

There are two types of inflation. Monetary inflation is an increase in the money supply that is higher than the increase in total real transactions (T), or the real amount of output measured by some fixed standard (like 1995 dollars in the example). Price inflation is a continuous increase in the price level. Note that the definition involves a continuing increase, since a one-time increase in the price level is technically not "inflation." It is possible, for example, for turnover to suddenly increase, resulting in greater MV, so with T unchanged, P will increase, but this one-time jump is not the same as chronic inflation, which is usually caused by monetary inflation. Inflation is measured using some price index, such as the consumer price index, producer price index, or the "GDP deflator" that uses prices throughout the economy.

Deflation is the opposite of inflation. With monetary deflation, there is a decrease in the money supply relative to goods, and with price deflation, there is a decrease in the price level. When people talk about "inflation" or "deflation" without any adjective, they usually mean price inflation or deflation. The "GDP deflator" is called that because price inflation increases the gross domestic product by more than the real increase in goods, and so the deflator index reduces or deflates the GDP to its real level relative to some base year.

With today's fiat money system controlled by central banks, the supply of money is determined by the policy of the government or its central bank. Governments profit from inflation, since the real value of its debt decreases, and it is able to repay bonds with "cheaper" money. Also, when newly created money is spent, the government or bank is able to get goods without having to produce anything. This revenue, called "seignorage," is effectively a tax on the total production of an economy. Also, inflation reduces the value of savings, so it is a tax on money holding or any loans, including bonds and savings accounts.

Monetary inflation does not raise all prices evenly. Some goods will rise in price more than others as the increase in money works its way unevenly through the economy. The subsequent distortion of relative prices is another bad effect from inflation.

In a pure market economy, there would be no government monopoly on the creation and holding of money. Most likely, free-market money would be based on and covertible to some commodity such as gold. So there would be little or no monetary inflation, and thus no price inflation other than minor fluctuations. As technology and increasing capital investments make production more efficient, some of that increased productivity would go to higher wages, some to higher land rent, and some to lower prices of goods. Hence, there would be a gradual reduction in the price level. This is in fact what happened during the 1800s when the world was on a gold standard and there was rapid technological change.

3. BANKING

A bank is a firm that receives deposits of money and loans the money. In most countries, banks pay interest to the depositors and charge a higher amount of interest to the borrowers, the difference in rates being kept for operating expenses, losses from bad loans, and profits. A bank is thus an "intermediary" or go-between. Ultimately, the lender is not the bank itself but the saver or depositor of the money. The bank is basically an agent that handles the lending, saving the depositor the trouble and risk of knocking on doors to see who wants to borrow his money.

In some cases, especially in Islamic countries, banks do not pay or receive direct interest, but instead participate as a partner in the business they loan money to, and get some of the profits. As noted in Chapter 5, there is always a "natural" interest rate when people save or borrow goods or money, due the time preference of preferring goods in the present rather than in the future. So in a profit-sharing partnership, the partner who borrows funds is in real effect paying interest, even though no financial interest is being paid. If you give someone an "interest-free" loan, and the going market rate is 5%, in effect the borrower is being given a gift of 5% annually; the borrower is really collecting the interest. Islamic law thus forbids direct payments of interest but does not rule out paying for the benefit of obtaining goods now and repaying later. The partnership approach may be a wise policy in general, since the bank as partner takes a business equity "interest" in seeing that the operation is successful.

One type of "bank" is a credit union, a club which receives deposits and loans money to its members. It is also possible to run a mutual exchange without cash, in which members exchange goods and services with debits and credit, account balances adding up to zero.

"Usury" means the collection of excessively high interest rates. This may happen when legal restrictions prevent the poor from obtaining credit from normal channels and instead have to borrow from loan sharks. In a pure market economy, there are no restrictions and thus usury does not exist. Interest paid for loans then reflects real risks as well as the natural interest rate and operating costs. Too-lenient laws on bankruptcy and fraud raise interest rates to borrowers, since they increase operating costs for bad loans not repaid. A pure market economy thus requires that fraud is severely prosecuted and that debts cannot be eliminated except by voluntary agreement.

"Credit" is the exchange of goods received in the present for goods paid back in the future. A person is said to have "credit" if he is able to receive goods today and can pay back later, plus interest. (A "credit" entry in bookkeeping has a different (and opposite!) meaning from that used in economics. You indicate a bookkeeping credit when you sell goods and receive cash.) Banks extend credit to borrowers, which means they enable borrowers to get goods at present and repay in the future. But in real effect, the banks being only intermediaries, the ultimate credit is extended by the depositors of the banks.

Money is a type of credit, since with the buyer obtains goods in the present and the seller does not get immediate goods but tickets for goods he will get in the future. Money is essentially transferable credit.

Banking is normally done with "fractional reserves." Reserves are stocks of money. They are fractional because only a fraction of deposits is kept by a bank, the rest being loaned out. Banks can therefore expand the money supply beyond the base of cash. You put $100 in the bank, and if the reserve ratio is 10%, the bank only keeps $10 in its vault, and loans out the other $90. It figures that it is unlikely for all depositors to come in and demand all their money at once. Central banks typically set reserve requirements for a country's banks.

This $90 loaned out gets deposited in some bank. That bank in turn keeps $9 and loans out the other $81. This goes on and on until out of the original $100, we now have $1000 of deposits created from all that lending if none of the extra money is held as cash. This is not a problem so long as 1) depositors are informed of the policy (hence it is not fraud), 2) they money loaned is eventually repaid; 3) there is little or no inflation of the cash base.

Unfortunately, conditions #2 and #3 have not been the case. Central banks have expanded the monetary base, which the banks then expand many times more through loans. Also, during recessions, many borrowers cannot repay their loans. Then many banks fail, since depositors are not able to get their cash back. The solution is not to eliminate fractional reserves (though some banks may do this and advertise themselves as extra-safe) but to eliminate conditions (2) and (3) by switching from coercive central banking to free banking.

With free banking and a pure and free market in money, the money supply expands with production and the demand for money, but no further, resulting in a stable money supply, without price inflation. There is no need for any government monetary policy, just as in a pure market economy there is no bread policy or automobile policy. Consumers and entrepreneurs can freely determine the demand and supply for both money and credit, just as with any other commodity. Bank safety is established by 1) banks wanting to have a reputation for security; 2) banks forming a clearing house and network for mutual support in case of crises; 3) private insurance; and 4) rating services that inform consumers of the various bank policies and risks.

With government deposit insurance, depositors may feel safe, but they are paying for this safety, since the banks must pay premiums for the insurance, and the government insurance can lead banks to take too-high risks and make unwise loans, as happened in the U.S. during the 1980s. The taxpayers had to pay many billions of dollars to bail out the savings and loans and banks. It turns out that this deposit insurance was very expensive indeed.

Under free banking, banks may be established without having to join a federal reserve or central bank system, and they may issue their own bank notes. There are no restrictions on interest rates or the extension of credit, so long as there is no fraud. Banks may form branches anywhere, making banking more accessible and efficient. Free banks are not required to have deposit insurance. There are also no taxes on savings, interest, banking, or bank notes. When the money consists of private bank notes (as it did in the U.S. before the Civil War, Scotland before 1844, and many other countries before the 20th century), monetary inflation does not take place. If one bank issues more notes than people want to hold, they take them to the bank for redemption, or conversion into some base money, such as gold. (For a detailed explanation of free banking, see *The Theory of Free Banking* by George Selgin.)

In a free economy, a government bank can operate, but not be imposed by force on the economy. It could provide services such as check clearing and the provision of currency in competition with other institutions. When all individuals have the freedom to use the currency of their choice, and when there is unhampered competition among financial institutions, then an economy will tend to have a stable currency, credit for responsible borrowers, and interest rates set by the desires and needs of enterprise. There is no need for government monetary policy other than the provision of a national currency that is offered to the public but not imposed by force.

Chapter 12: The Business Cycle

1. THE NATURE OF THE BUSINESS CYCLE

A cycle is a pattern that repeats either exactly or approximately over time. Market economies have experienced what are called "business" or "trade" cycles. Business conditions, including total output, employment, and profits, experience booms, times of growth and prosperity, and busts, times of decline and depressed conditions. When charted over time, the variables resemble a sine wave, the top half of a circle followed by the bottom half.

There are various names for the phases of the cycle. The bottom is called a depression or trough. It is followed by an upswing, called an expansion. The first part of the upswing is a recovery, and the second part, if it is steeply rising, is called a boom. The top is called a peak. If the following decline is very steep, it is a crash (the economy crashes). The downswing is called a recession (to recede means to go back or down).

Since this cycle resembles a sine wave, going up and then down, with a curved top and bottom, it has some interesting mathematical properties. Wait a minute! Don't roll your eyes! I will try to make the math as simple as possible. Math, after all, is just logic written in a different language. As a logical person, you can follow the math if it is presented gradually and clearly.

If you draw a straight line on paper, it has a slope. Suppose it is a line drawn diagonally to the right, starting at the lower left and going to the upper right. The slope tells us how steeply the line is rising. It is calculated by making two points on the line and then drawing a horizontal line from the bottom point towards the right and from the top line down until it meets the horizontal line. (If this is new to you, try it with paper and pencil.) Now measure the length of the vertical line and the horizontal line (from their meeting point to the diagonal line). Then divide the vertical line by the horizontal line. This number is the slope. If it equals one, the line has a 45 degree angle. If the slope is bigger than one, the diagonal line is steep; if less than one, the line has a low slope.

If a line is not straight, then the slope changes along the line. The slope can be seen by drawing a straight line at a point which is tangent to it, which means that if you come to the line from the perpendicular to it, you are also coming perpendicularly to the line, perpendicular meaning at right angles.

Now here is the punch line of this little mathematical excursion. Let's start at a depression. The slope of the cycle is zero—in the small neighborhood of the bottom, it is nearly a horizontal line. That's because the economy is no longer declining but also not yet arisen. When the economy recovers, the cycle is headed diagonally upward, and the slope becomes positive. As the cycle line continues upward, the slope becomes steeper and steeper as the recover gets faster and faster.

But somewhere along the expansion, the line stops getting steeper and becomes less steep. It still slopes up, but the tangent line, the slope, becomes shallower and shallower until at the peak, it is horizontal again, growth having slowed to a halt. That point where the slope changed from increasing in steepness to decreasing in steepness is called the "inflection point."

Which is a very important point! Because even though during the recovery, all variables are headed up—output, employment, profits, are still increasing vigorously—the change in the slope means that from now on, the rate of increase will slow down. The steepness will decrease. The expansion is already doomed just when things look best! As Henry George (1879, p. 542) stated, in a different context, "When the sun passes the meridian, it can be told only by the way the short shadows fall; for the heat of the day yet increases."

Do you see the importance of the slope? The puzzling thing about business cycles is why an economy that is doing so great comes to a screeching halt and then declines. But if the slope has started to decrease already during the boom, we can see that the reason the economy peaked out is that the change in slope turned negative already during the boom at the point of inflection.

Now we need to answer the question: why did the slope change? Why can't the economy just keep going up and up and up, or at least stay at a peak, forever?

2. THEORIES OF BUSINESS CYCLES

Economists, puzzled by depressions, have come up with many different "theories" or explanations for them. They can be divided into two types: real and financial. A real theory means that real factors such as changes in supply or demand are the causes. Financial factors mean that the cause is a change in the amount of money or prices. It is generally agreed that most of these "theories" or hypotheses have not explained cycles very well.

Most of the reporting and analysis of the mortgage problems since 2007 focused on the lending practices and the policies governing mortgages and their derivatives as the proximate causes of the economic crisis that began in 2007 and intensified in 2008. For example, some analysts have pointed to the Community Reinvestment Acts of 1977 and 1995 that required banks to lend to low-income communities which had higher risks. When conditions such as escalating real estate prices are ripe for a substantial increase in mortgage loans, these acts contributed to a greater increase in subprime mortgages by lenders such as Countrywide Bank than would otherwise have been the case.

The size of the mortgage losses were exacerbated by the secondary market promoted mostly by the government sponsored enterprises Fannie Mae and Freddie Mac, which could borrow funds backed by an implicit government guarantee that became explicit. By the end of 2007, the liabilities and guarantees of these two GSEs were equal to the U.S. federal debt (Norberg, 2009, pp. 42–3).

But the deeper issue is why the real estate boom occurred in the first place. The expansion of real estate construction and increase in prices after 2001 was not an isolated phenomenon, but has to be seen in the context of a real estate boom-bust cycle which has been occurring in the U.S. for two hundred years (Foldvary 1997, Foldvary 2007).

We will not delve into all these hypotheses, but concentrate on two which fit the facts better than the others. One is financial and the other emphasizes real factors. When we put the two together, we get a full explanation of business cycles and how to stop them.

The real-factor theory was first discovered by Henry George, who recognized the key role played by real estate in bringing a boom to a halt.

George (1879) noted that depressions were preceded by booms accompanied by land speculation, "followed by symptoms of checked production" (p. 268). The major barrier to production becomes the high cost of land and rent, in effect "a lockout of labor and capital by landowners" (p. 270). Speculative land costs demand a part of future output in the present. George's theory attempted to resolve the paradox of idle labor and capital in the depths of a depression. The reason the market was not clearing was that labor and capital were cut off from the necessary natural opportunities offered by land.

Writing after the depression of the 1870s, George pointed to the example of the railroads, the construction of which had been accompanied by widespread speculation that "ran up land values in every direction ... Lots on the outskirts of San Francisco rose hundreds and thousands per cent, and farming land was taken up and held for high prices" (p. 276). As the transcontinental railroad approached completion, instead of bringing prosperity, a depression began. The rapid construction of railroads itself was a result of land grants by the federal government to spur on a national rail network. The train of events that contributed to the depression of the 1870s was therefore not a pure market process but induced to a great extent by the shock of infrastructure subsidies by government, capitalized into land values which then increased via speculation to heights which choked off enterprise.

To examine George's theory, let's start at the depression or trough. Due to low demand and high vacancies due to bankruptcies and cutbacks, commercial rent and land prices are at rock bottom. The downward spiral has ended, as most fragile and badly-invested ventures have already gone bankrupt. Now the stronger enterprises start expanding again, helped by low prices of labor, real estate, and interest rates. While demand rises (demand curves shift to the right), prices during the recovery are usually steady, since there is a large supply of idle resources.

As the expansion progresses, an upward spiral is set in motion, since greater employment implies greater spending, stimulating more enterprise. Now vacancies in real estate become low, and prices and rents start rising. A boom in the construction of buildings begins, stimulating the demand for land. The recovery becomes a boom. The rate of increase, or slope, of the upswing is at its maximum. Speculators now enter the market, since they anticipate higher future prices for real estate. They drive the price of land even higher. Much of the real estate construction is also speculative, as builders expect their land value to rise and contribute to profits.

But now enterprises find that the price of real estate is higher than that warranted for present-day use, since it reflects future expectations. "The invisible barrier but for which buildings would rise and the city would spread, is the high price of land, a price that increases the more certainly it is seen that a growing population needs the land" (George, 1883, p. 126). Adam Smith's invisible hand is blocked by George's invisible barrier. There are of course other increasing costs, such as interest rates, raw materials, and labor, but speculation is an especially powerful price-increasing force for land.

Enterprises slow down their expanding. We have reached the inflection point. Even though enterprises are still expanding rapidly, the rate of expansion has slowed down due to the too-high price of real estate. Contributing to the slow-down are higher prices for labor and other inputs as well, but these have not increased nearly as much, because only with land does an increase in demand fall fully on an increase in price—because the supply of land in a given area cannot be expanded, unlike other inputs!

The slowdown in real-estate construction spreads to other industries, as, for example, less furniture is ordered and less steel and lumber is demanded. Industries producing such capital goods, which expanded rapidly, now contract. Workers laid off or working fewer hours spend less. The rate of increase in the economy slows even more, until the slope becomes horizontal—growth has halted. The economy is at its peak, but is now headed for a fall! Because the growth rate has been decreasing, and now turns negative.

When investors realize growth has stopped, many will want to unload stocks, and a crash in the stock market often heralds the coming depression. But that's only the beginning, and only a symptom of the problem, not the originating cause, although the loss of stock value contributes to the decline, since those who have lost their financial wealth will no longer spend money on large items.

The recession feeds on itself, as lower output leads to lower income and to lower spending, which reduces output even more. Real estate prices have remained at a plateau even though vacancies have increased, because the owners don't wish to sell below peak prices. This phenomenon repeats itself each cycle! But eventually, increasing bankruptcies result in lower rentals for landlords, and some of those with negative cash flows must sell. Prices now start tumbling down. Many landlords go broke, not being able to pay their mortgages. In many cases, the debts of real-estate owners are greater than the value of their properties. Loans are not being repaid, and banks are losing great amounts of money. Many banks fail.

After the crash, bankruptcies and cutbacks slow down, and the rate of decrease becomes less steep. This is the second inflection point, where the economy is still shrinking, but the change in the rate of growth has become positive—the decreases become less steep. The economy is receding, headed towards a trough. In the depression, many resources, especially labor and real estate, are idle, and prices are low. But the decrease has ended—growth is flat again, and the change in the rate is positive as old and new businesses take advantage of low prices to expand again.

But this is only half the story. We need to go further into the second half, involving the financial sector. As stated by Friedrich Hayek (1933, p. 90), "Although there is no doubt that all nonmonetary Trade Cycle theories tacitly assume that the production of capital goods has been made possible by the creation of new credit, … no one has yet proved that this circumstance should form the exclusive basis of the explanation."

The real estate that was bought by enterprises and speculators during the boom was gotten using borrowed money. We need to see what was happening with the banking system.

One scenario described by the Austrian school of economics, especially by Friedrich Hayek (1933), starts with the injection of money into the economy by the banking system, especially nowadays by a central bank. During a depression, it is common for central banks such as the U.S. Federal Reserve System to increase the money supply to stimulate growth and bring about a quicker recovery. The money supply might also be increased to accommodate a real-estate boom. Whatever the cause, the extra money has the same temporary effect as extra savings. With more loanable funds, interest rates drop, or they do not rise as much as they normally would during a recovery.

Enterprises producing higher-order capital goods, used by other industries, are especially sensitive to interest rates, since their investments need to be very long term. These firms borrow money to expand. But this is a phony expansion, since the low interest rate is artificial and temporary. As prices rise due to the expanded money, either the money supply must stop its artificial increase, or else the inflation will accelerate as people anticipate ever higher prices and react by increasing prices and wages even more. The decrease in money expansion creates "tight" credit, and interest rates increase, bringing to a halt the expansion of interest-sensitive firms, including especially real-estate construction.

Without the money injection, interest rates would rise anyway due to increased demand for loans for real-estate speculation. So the monetary factor and rise in interest rates work together with the rise in land prices to increase the costs of new investments and lower their returns. Both these cause bring about the inflection point during the boom, when the rate of increase slows. Thus it is that during the height of the boom, the economy is already doomed. The cause of the bust is the previous boom.

3. ELIMINATING THE BUSINESS CYCLE

Business cycles are economically wasteful and cause misery to those thrown out of work. Millions of lives are disrupted. Moreover, during a phony boom, resources are diverted to projects that turn out to be wasted—such as shopping centers that stand half vacant for years. It is recognized by governments at least that recessions are unpopular, but they attempt to treat only the symptoms and effects of the cycle, such as "stimulating" the economy, a stimulus that can be ill timed and only offer temporary artificial relieve, often hurting the economy later.

If indeed the major causes of the cycles are the real-estate speculative booms and the artificial increases in the money supply, the remedy is to stop both events. The artificial increase in money supply can be halted permanently by implementing free banking. Without a central bank and a national currency imposed on the economy, inflation of the money supply beyond the growth of the economy is no longer feasible, since there is no longer a monopoly of the money supply, as discussed in Chapter 11.

This leaves us with the real-estate boom. But land gets its value from future rents, speculators anticipating increased rent. When most or all this rent is collected by the government or by communities, it knocks the legs out of land speculation, because all the future gain is collected away. Real estate prices and rents then only reflect current use, not expected future uses. The absence of land speculation also reduces the demand for loans, so interest rates are not so high. With both interest rates and real estate prices determined by current enterprise, the expansion does not develop into an unsustainable boom.

The remedy, then, for business cycles consists of the public collection of rent—and free banking. Free banking will dampen the cycles somewhat, but both together will eliminate the major cycles. Shorter minor cycles can still arise, but they will not produce the massive unemployment and bankruptcies that have plagued the U.S. and Europe since 1800. In a pure market economy, growth can still be uneven as technology develops new products in spurts, but the world-wide massive cycles will become history. Eliminate the cause, and the effect will vanish.

Chapter 13: Environmental Economics

The environment consists of natural resources which contribute to our well being by their very existence, rather than by being used up. These resources are of two types: renewable, such as wildlife and water, and non-renewable, such as oil and minerals. Environmental economics consists of the utility gained by using resources, including the differentiation of short-run and long-run utilities, the maximization of the utilities from a stock of resources, the calculation of benefits and costs, the property rights associated with natural resources, and ways of paying for using and abusing the environment.

In Chapter 1 it was shown that the Universal Ethic endows humanity with the common ownership of natural resources. This ownership does not consist of all rights to natural resources, but the right to their benefits, which is economically manifested in land rent.

1. MINERALS

The use of non-renewable resources such as minerals necessarily involves the using up of the materials. The problem of the scarcity of non-renewable resources is resolved automatically by the free market. As a resource gets used up and becomes increasingly reduced in supply, its price will increase. This higher cost will induce the users of the resource to economize on its use, including recycling it if possible, and also to seek out substitutes. The higher the price, the less of the good will be demanded, and so as supplies become used up more and more, the ever higher price will induce less usage.

With a community, ultimately humanity, considered the proper owner of the rents of natural resources, there are three basic ways of obtaining the rent. The first is "ex ante" or prior to mining. A company bids and pays for the opportunity or franchise of both the exploration and extraction of the oil or minerals. The second method is "ex post" or after mining. The firm pays a fee based on the amount of resource extracted (e.g. per ton). This is also called a "severence" charge. The third way, also after mining, is to take a percentage of the profits from the operation. None of the methods by itself takes the rent or accurately measures it, since in mining it is not easy to separate the rent from the entrepreneurial profit, so a combination of the three is usually the best way to obtain the rent.

Liquid resources, such as water and oil, pose an extra problem, since if for example an underground water supply is divided among several plots of land, each owner will want to drain away as much as possible, since the loss is borne by all the owners together. An extraction fee is therefore needed to prevent such exploitation.

2. RENEWABLE RESOURCES

Renewable resources do not need to be used up, so their economics is different. The sustainable use of a resource, such that the same amount or greater remains for future use, does not have a scarcity rent, although it can have a locational rent. The using up of the resource does involve a scarcity rent and should have a charge, as with non-renewable resources, but in this case, there can be damage to future generations because some resources do not have an established market and because many of the wildlife resources are very fragile and endangered.

Much of this destruction is often not the result of market processes but is caused by subsidies. For example, agricultural subsidies induce farmers to cultivate marginal land that would otherwise be left in a natural state. This land is typically artificially fertilized, so not only does wildlife habitat get destroyed but more pollution is created by protectionist policy.

3. POLLUTION

The oceans and the atmosphere are a type of common pool, although we can also separate out some local pollution. Since the oceans are part of our natural resources, or economic land, those who dump pollutants into the seas are obtaining a benefit from the use of this land, and thus gain a rent. Humanity as the owner of the oceans and atmosphere is therefore entitled to collect this rent, which ideally would compensate all future generations for the damages. Charging a fee for pollution also compensates humanity for the damage done, as is required by the market process. However, it is difficult to estimate the amount of damage committed by the pollution of a large area such as the upper atmosphere or the Gulf of Mexico oil spill disaster of 2010, especially since the damage lasts into the indefinite future.

The central problem is that the government policy has not marketized most of our air and water, either making it private or charging rent. Users and abusers of the environment have not paid for the social cost, the damage being done to health and the preservation of the global climate. By treating the atmosphere and oceans as free goods, there was no incentive to protect it. Even when the polluter pays for the clean up, usually they have not had to compensate society for the full social costs. Municipalities also are able to use rivers and oceans as dumps for sewage.

The ideal solution is to have the polluter pay for the use of the environmental service. The "polluter pays principle" was adopted by the OECD, the Organization for Economic Cooperation and Development, in 1974. This intergovernmental organization recognized that the marketization of the environment requires an international agreement, so that firms which use costly anti-pollution devices do not suffer a competitive disadvantage. A pollution charge would also encourage inventions and investments in anti-pollution technology and in less-polluting techniques such as solar energy.

Some proposed environmental taxes do not directly charge for pollution, but for products whose usage is currently polluting. For example, "carbon tax" has been proposed, based on the carbon content of the fuel used: a higher charge for coal than for oil and a lower one still for natural gas. But this is more directly a tax on consumption. It is economically more efficient and morally less coercive to place a charge directly on the pollutant, such as carbon monoxide, in proportion to its damage. Such a charge would not be a tax in substance, but a rent and fee for the use of environmental land.

There are at least three ways to set such a pollution charge. The first method is to measure the economic impact of environmental damage, and set the charge equal to that cost.

For example, air or noise pollution can reduce real-estate values. When direct measurements are not available, one can use the demand revelation approach. People are asked either what they would pay for an environmental benefit or what they are willing to receive as compensation for some reduction in environmental quality.

The second method is to assume that the total damage from pollution is infinite (considering the effects on future generations for all time to come), so any amount charged will but compensate a little for the damage. The charge is then determined by budgetary desires. The total amount of revenue obtained can be a budget residual or difference. Suppose the total budget is B, and the revenues obtained from site rents and mineral extractions and other rents is R. If R is less than B, then the total pollution charges can be B - R. We then designate a list of pollutants and their relative damage per ton, adding up the total ton-damage. We then divide the amount of funds to raise (B – R) by the ton-damage to get the charge per ton.

Suppose that B – R is $1 million. We have two pollutants, chlorine and arsenic, each consisting of 100 tons per year. Arsenic is nine times as damaging as chlorine (as a hypothetical example). The total ton-damage is 100 (for the chlorine) + 9*100 (for the arsenic) = 1000. The charge per ton is $1 million divided by 1000, which equals $1000. So chlorine would be charged $1000 per ton and arsenic $9000 per ton. The effect of the charge would be to reduce the pollution, and so the fee per ton could be increased the next period, which would then reduce pollution even more.

The third way to charge would be to treat the ocean or atmosphere as private property, and maximize the revenue for dumping into it. For example, suppose some corporation were assigned ownership of the North Atlantic ocean, with rights to collect fees for pollution dumping. The firm would set the rates per pollutant, given some list of pollutants and relative charges by a governing authority. It would try to maximize its profits and would set a rate that would most likely be so high it would substantially reduce the pollution. This company in turn would pay its rent, which would be most of its revenues, to some governing authority, such as the United Nations, providing it an independent source of revenues. If the revenue is greater than the budget of the agency, the funds could be distributed to the member nations. To keep the process efficient and honest, provision should be made for members to be able to secede from the organization and form alternative international organizations which would also share this rent.

A combination of these methods would include the natural environment in a global market economy, so that the social costs of enterprise would be borne by those obtaining the benefits.

Chapter 14: Economic Growth, Development, and Population

1. ENVIRONMENTAL EFFECTS OF POPULATION

Population merits a separate chapter because one of the major social phenomena today is the rapid increase in the human population on earth, and secondly, because the effects of the increase are controversial due to its complexity. The figures for population growth are indeed startling. From 1990 to 2025, the world's population will have increased by 3.2 billion, with projections that the peak will be from 11 to 14 billion people. However, figures on their own do not tell us the full story.

We can begin by separating the environmental from the purely economic effects.

The environmental effects, keeping other things equal are largely negative. First, human populations crowd out wildlife, destroying its habitat and competing for sites and food. Secondly, with more people there is greater competition for areas of natural beauty, which are mostly fixed in supply. There is only one Yosemite National Park, and only so many miles of good beaches. More people implies either greater crowding or else a higher entrance fee.

The effects on wildlife can be dealt with by, first, establishing wilderness reserves where there is little or no human activity other than camping. This can be done both by government and by private initiative, by buying and preserving land, as the Nature Conservancy and other conservation organizations are doing. If there is the public collection of rent, then such reserves would also pay the rent charge, but the government in turn would spend that rent on the reserve, to preserve it, so the payments can cancel out.

In addition, as noted in Chapter 13, any destruction or using up of wildlife and the world's genetic endowment would be subject to a charge, which would reduce the damage. Another approach would be to also permit the private ownership of wildlife, such as whales, and then the owners would be legally entitled to compensation for any destruction of the wildlife and would receive the revenue from its sale. Humanity as a whole or some community would also have a residual ownership, so the owners themselves would be subject to charges for the destruction of wildlife and habitat.

2. THE ECONOMICS OF POPULATION

The general belief persists that wage levels, especially in the less developed countries, are the result of a population that is growing too fast.

Thomas Malthus fathered the doom-laden demography thesis: that unrestrained population growth leads to poverty and hunger. His conjecture was that population tends to grow geometrically, since with a certain percentage annual population growth, it keeps doubling in the same time period. But, according to his projection, the growth of agriculture is arithmetic, growing by the same absolute amount during each time period. For example, population may grow like 10, 20, 40, 80, while agriculture grows like 10, 20, 30, 40. Without birth control, population runs into the limits of natural resources and gets controlled by deaths.

David Ricardo contributed to the explanation: an increase in population will lead to migration to lands with lower productivity, lowering wages, as discussed in Chapter 2. Henry George pointed out that the land tenure system also affects the margin of production, since if land is used suboptimally, the margin will be less productive than needed for that population. But George went beyond this to show that the Malthusian scenario does not necessarily hold. An increase in population can also have increasing returns, boosting per-capita output with better organization and a finer division of labor. More knowledge and technology can be used, as greater populations result in economies of scale with mass production.

If the earth were running out of natural resources, the price of commodities such as metals and grains would be increasing. Instead, their prices relative to manufactured goods has decreased. Population has negative effects on the natural environment, but it is by itself not necessarily an economic problem. Also, the evidence shows that as people become wealthier, they tend to want fewer children, so the best antidote to excessive population growth is economic growth that increases family incomes.

3. ECONOMIC GROWTH AND DEVELOPMENT

Economic growth is an increase in the total output in an economy. Economic development is an increase in the material standard of living in an economy or an increase in the capital goods of an area. Development is usually measured as per-capita gross domestic or national product, but if the development is highly unequal, per-capita income can increase without affecting much of the population. A more refined measurement of economic development is per-capita income divided by an inequality index, such as those discussed in Chapter 9.

Three key problems in less-developed countries (LDCs) are poverty, unemployment, and environmental destruction. Out of the gross global product of US $20 trillion (thousand thousand million) in 1990, less than $3.4 trillion was generated in less-developed countries (Todaro, 1994, p. 39). Agriculture has been measured as 35 times more productive in North America as in Asia and Africa (p. 51). The elimination of these gaps is the principle aim of economic development. There are also internal gaps in many LDCs, which often have a more modern sector in the cities and a more traditional, lower-wage agricultural sector.

The conventional theory of economic development centers around growth models which emphasize the additions to the stock of capital goods. There is some capital-output ratio, $k = K/Y$, so that a certain increase in capital goods K will induce an increase in output Y. There is also some proportion s of national output that is saved and therefore invested rather than consumed. Therefore, the growth rate (annual change in Y divided by Y) is equal to s / k, the proportion of income or output saved (s) divided by k. The implication is that development depends on how much capital is added each year.

Much developmental aid followed this theory, pumping massive amounts of capital into the Third World to build dams, roads, steel mills, factories, as well as machinery, resulting in colossal national debts to foreign banks and international lending agencies such as the International Monetary Fund and the World Bank. The problem, of course, is that capital goods are heterogenous, and there is no uniform capital/output ratio. A gigantic dam will also disrupt the lives of hundreds of villages, destroy forests, and flood a great deal of farm land, and its expected life is often far less than originally projected, due to its filling up with silt. Many of these projects, being government to government, are subject to political influences at both ends, not to speak of funds being siphoned to corruption. Also, capital goods require complementary human capital, skills in using them. But a key problem in this model is also that it omits the role played by land in development.

The causes of these problems in LDCs are the same as in the more-developed countries (MDCs), but more evident due to the prominence of primary industries: agriculture, fishing, and mining. The typical land tenure in LDCs is the ownership of much of the land as large estates by a few land owning families, who are closely connected with the military and government. The farmers typically rent or own small plots of land, and often must supplement their subsistence crops with income earned in commercial plantations, where coffee, bananas, and other crops are grown for export. Women are usually dominated by men, who control much of the property. Wars, and civil strife, and oppression have made sheer survival the main priority of many of the people in these countries, as malfunctioning economies feed political instability, which then prevents development.

LDCs have less capital and less technology, but this can be remedied by investment. But the governments of most LDCs have placed barriers against investment. High taxes, legal restrictions, complicated permit requirements, and massive bureaucratic procedures have stifled domestic and foreign enterprise. Often, corrupt government officials require a bribe to obtain a permit. Some governments impose costly and time-consuming visa requirements for foreign visitors, or make travel impossible. Unemployment in LDCs as in MDCs is caused by such barriers between labor and resources. In many cases, people are not officially listed as employed, but work anyway in the informal or underground economy, without paying taxes and bribes or getting permits.

In Eastern Europe and in some LDCs, organized crime plagues enterprise, making businesses pay protection money. The government, including members of the police and border guards, are often allied with the racketeers and share in the loot. A truly free economy cannot be established unless such crime and looting is rooted out.

As explained in Chapters 2 and 9, poverty is caused by low wages at the margin of production—low productivity on the worst land being used. The remedy is to both increase productivity at this margin and to move the margin towards more productive land. The community collection of the land rent will induce the most productive use of land, so that the margin will be at the best available unused land. The removal of taxation on labor and enterprise will then enable workers to keep the full product of their labor and will encourage investment in more productive enterprise. The removal of restrictions will also enable farmers and small business persons to obtain credit and create enterprises.

Those countries which have developed have had relatively free-market oriented policies grounded initially in land reform. Japan in the 19th century and Taiwan after 1950 removed the old aristocracy and turned land over to the farmers, combined with a substantial tax on the land rent. As Fred Harrison (1983, p. 154) states, "within two decades Japan had completed the transition to modern economic growth and was ready to take on all comers!" Land rent was used to develop the infrastructure, which further increased productivity and rent. Funds from agriculture were used to develop export-oriented industry. This is essentially the economic model and theory of the French physiocrats of the 1700s (see Chapter 19), who originated the first model of economic development, a model that in its essential elements has had the best actual success.

The engine of development is the desire of individuals to improve their lives. The prerequisite to development is therefore the establishment of a pure market economy, where labor has equal access to natural resources and is able to keep its product, thus having the incentive to invest much of it for future gains. With freedom also will come a sea of foreign investment seeking the most productive fields.

And of course, those peoples who do not wish to change their way of life, particularly the primal and tribal peoples in the rain forests and the nomads of the deserts and dwellers of the Arctic—they have the right to continue their cultures unmolested by the onslaught of commercial nature-wreaking development. Human beings did not start out poor, hungry, needing development. Primal man had natural wealth from the bounty of nature. Only after humanity turned to agriculture and conquerors took the land did the brave hunter become a lowly peasant working for a wage pittance from dawn to dusk while the lord dined on wine and game hens under chandeliers. Only after the descent to serfdom does development beckon with the promise of increasing productivity. And then, unless workers are liberated from bureaucracy and taxation, and unless the yields of land are shared by the community, the road of development will be a long, hot, stony journey.

Chapter 15: Governance and Public Choice

1. GOVERNANCE

"Governance" consists of the enforcement of rules. A "government" is most generally an agency which enforces rules. We normally think of a government as that of a state, which is a government having ultimate authority over some geographic area and over its subjects or citizens. But a voluntary association also has governance, which we can call an "association" to distinguish it from a state.

The state government can play two different economic roles. The first role is that of marketization: the legal recognition of the rules and rights of the market and their enforcement. The fundamental ethical rules that markets adhere to were discussed in Chapter 1. Marketization involves the implementation of the following rules:

1. All acts and only those acts which coercively harm others are prohibited or penalized. Every individual has the natural and legal right to life, liberty, and property. This includes the right to create voluntary associations.
2. Contracts consist of voluntary agreements. If an agreement is violated, the victim may sue for damages.
3. People and enterprises that are not able to pay obligations may declare bankruptcy. This does not eliminate the debt, but provides for an orderly priority of payment and the ability of the debtor to preserve the minimal possessions required for life.
4. Property rights and boundaries are established and recorded. These include air rights and the division of the electro-magnetic spectrum into frequencies for radio, telephone, and television transmissions.

5. The possession of natural resource properties, including surface land, minerals, air rights, and pollution dumps, are subject to the payment of the rents and social costs involved in using these properties.

These fundamental market rules are best inscribed in a constitution. A constitution consists of the supreme rules of a community, such that all other laws and rules are based on the constitutional rules. The constitution sets the organization of the government, the rules that the members follow, and the rights that the members and visitors have. There is a branch of economics called "constitutional economics" which studies the different effects of having various constitutional rules.

The second role that government plays is intervention. In contrast to marketization, intervention is an interference into the market process, making the economy less efficient and violating rather than protecting rights. Whether policy is marketizing or interventionist depends on the incentives of public choice.

2. PUBLIC CHOICE

A private choice is a decision that only affects the person who does the choosing. When a decision affects others, the choice becomes public. In particular, when people vote or when government officials select policies, these are public choices. Political scientists have studied these decisions, but economists also have studied political choices. This has become a branch of economics called "public choice."

Two of the key issues in public choice involves voting by the citizens and the choices made by government officials. In the democracies we have today, citizens are confronted by candidates and parties seeking the votes of thousands and millions of people. These candidates are total strangers to most voters. As noted by Henry George (1883, p. 174), "a principle should always be kept in mind which we have largely ignored, that the people cannot manage details, nor intelligently choose more than a few officials." An individual voter not only does not know the character of the candidate, but also knows little about the candidate's past political record, how he or she voted on various issues and what kinds of interests have influenced the candidate. Most people are busy with their private lives and don't find it a high priority to invest much time in researching the background of a candidate, since one vote will normally make very little difference in the outcome.

Hence, most voters have what economists call "rational ignorance," a lack of knowledge about candidates and issues due to the lack of power make a difference in the outcome. Also, many people are swayed by emotional appeals and the image and appearance of a candidate, how he or she appears on television.

As a result, candidates must project a positive image and appeal to the voters' emotions and ideologies. They get the most votes by appealing the majority views, not to fringe and minority interests. Given a one-dimensional range of views on a particular issues, such as spending a little, a moderate amount, or much on the military, the voter in the middle of the distribution is called the "median voter." Candidates will appeal to this voter, since appealing to the right or left of the median will lose more votes than it gains. Thus, in a two-party system, the parties will tend to converge on the views of the median voters. Much of the advertising will then be to project an image of good character and to vilify the opponent. The two-party system in the United States has become a duopoly, or dual monopoly, with laws in most states imposing burdensome signatory requirement for minor parties. With proportional representation, where people vote for parties and minority interests can be represented, the candidates are selected by the party leaders, leaving the voters to choose among parties offering packages of policies which they may not like entirely.

To appeal to thousands and millions of voters, candidates and parties need to spend great amounts of money, unless the law restricts it and provides for media access. The funds for campaigns comes from individuals, special interests, and the government.

In large campaigns, the bulk of the funds come from special interests rather than individuals. Unless a voter has a good deal of sympathy with a candidate, party, or issue, he will not tend to pay much attention to politics. The reason is that the benefits to an individual are small, compared to the cost in time and resources, unless he is keenly interested. In contrast, special interests, such as farmers, captains of industry, and religious organizations, receive concentrated benefits from government subsidies, protection, and privileges. They therefore have a strong incentive both to contribute to campaigns to gain influence, and then after the election to lobby for favorable legislation. The public choices of legislators are therefore heavily influenced by special interests. Since candidate need funds and votes, they cater to special interests and the median voter. The interests of minorities without financial or voting clout will usually be ignored.

Non-elected government officials also make public choices. As James Buchanan has noted, their choices are "cost-influencing" but not "cost influenced." This means that bureaucrats make rules that impose costs on others, but the officials themselves do not have any cost. The head of a government agency will normally seek to increase his power and authority and spend as much as possible.

The result of these choices by government officials is that much government spending is geared to the desires of special interests and of officials rather than the goods that the public desires. This is a main reason for government failure. The other major reason is the knowledge problem—that even with good intentions and incentives, a central government lacks the knowledge needed to plan for large economic activities.

Henry George analyzed the impact on public choice of the economic structure of society, of the effect of democracy when there is a great inequality in wealth.

Political equality is not sufficient to promote prosperity and avoid decline. "Equality of political rights will not compensate for the denial of the equal right to the bounty of nature" (1879, p. 545). If the equal right to vote co-exists with an increasing economic inequality, a large class of poor and a small land-owning elite, this "must ultimately beget either the despotism of organized tyranny or the worse despotism" of chaotic revolt (p. 530). The slaughter and wars in Rwanda, Cambodia, El Salvador, Bosnia, and elsewhere testify to the terrible consequences of the failure to establish a just economic and political order.

George recognized the important distinction between form and substance in government and economics: "forms are nothing when substance has gone, and the forms of popular government are those from which the substance of freedom may most easily go" (p. 530). Citizens may still vote, yet the vote can be empty as power passes "into the hands of jobbers who will buy and sell it" or "into the hands of demagogues who will seize and wield it" (p. 531).

Democracy degenerates when there is a gross inequality of wealth, poisoning the national character. "To give the suffrage to tramps, to paupers, to men to whom the chance to labor is a boon, to men who must beg, or steal, or starve, is to invoke destruction … To put political power in the hands of men embittered and degraded by poverty is … to put out the eyes of a Samson and to twine his arms around the pillars of national life." Thus, "in a corrupt democracy the tendency is always to give power to the worst … the worst float to the top, … transmuting races of freemen into races of slaves" (p. 532). "A corrupt government must finally corrupt the people, and when the people become corrupt there is no resurrection" (pp. 532–3).

George saw in his day what we recognize too well in ours, that it is in our great cities that is found "the greatest wealth and the deepest poverty. And it is here that popular government has most clearly broken down …" Here "are men of power, whose favor the ambitious must court and whose vengeance he must avoid" (p. 533).

3. GOVERNMENT STRUCTURE

The implication of public choice analysis is that 1) a precondition for a sound government is a sound economy, in which gross inequalities, due to the unequal ownership of land, are avoided, and 2) the efficient provision of collective services is best left to the market process or, if that is not feasible, that government be structured so that the incentive to confer privileges is minimized.

The structure of government needs to be inscribed in a constitution, so that it is not easy to change by legislation. These constitutional restraints are of two types: 1) restraints on government activity; 2) the division of government power.

Restraints on government include a general rule that government shall not restrict peaceful and honest action. Government must also be prevented from imposing taxes and arbitrary costs. A further restraint is that government be voluntary. Secession from a government jurisdiction is allowed from services such as education and local public works, and from the authority of the government itself. People could then form alternative associations and deduct the cost of substitute services from their taxes or assessments to government.

A division of government power includes horizontal and vertical divisions. The horizontal division is the well-known separation of powers at some level of government, such as a federal government. The usual division is into a legislature (parliament or congress), an executive (president, monarch, and/or prime minister), and a judicial branch, each with partial independence with an ability to affect the actions of the others. One possible fourth branch is an agency responsible for elections.

A vertical division of government power consists of levels of government, from local to federal. The United States has three levels: federal, state, and tribal for Native American Indians and aboriginal Alaskans. Cities and county governments are actually agents of the states, and only have powers granted to them by the states. Vertical division can be increased by allowing individuals to secede from any jurisdiction and create alternative governance. Many private communities are already providing services similar to those of government (see Foldvary, 1994).

The benefit of vertical division is that governance becomes more of a market. With decentralized governance, people can more easily move and join communities with more efficient governance or with specialized services. Bad government becomes less likely if people can secede from it rather than have to engage in costly and unlikely reforms.

Another aspect of government structure is the method of public choice by the voters. As described above, when candidates must appeal to thousands of anonymous voters, there is a strong incentive for special interests to be influential. An alternative is bottom-up voting. A city or county is divided into townships and then into districts of about 500 persons. Each district elects a local council. Each council then elects a representative to the township board, representing about a dozen districts. The townships then elect delegates to a city or county council. These elect the members of the state legislature, which in turn elects members to the federal congress or parliament. At the bottom level, the districts are small enough for the voters to know the candidates personally, so there are no media campaigns and appeals to image. Special interests would find it difficult to sway the elections. Bottom-up democracy is an alternative to the top-down systems that have been an improvement over dictatorships but have let to the rule of special interests and a top-heavy government.

A free and prosperous economy requires governance with a marketizing rather than interventionist policy. The government needs to be carefully structured so that the incentive for government monopolies, privileges, and oppression is minimized. This is done with constitutional rules which restrain government intervention, provide for the collection of rents, and allow individuals to exit from jurisdictions when government becomes abusive.

Chapter 16: Public Goods and Public Finance

1. PUBLIC GOODS

The public consists of two or more persons. If an economic goods is being used by two or more persons at the same time, it is a public good, otherwise it is private. Public goods are also called collective goods. For example, if you eat a sandwich, it is a private good, since it is going into your mouth and nobody else's. On the other hand, if you and a friend are watching one television, the TV is a public good. Clearly, the same object can be private or collective depending on its use at a particular time, since if you later watch the TV alone, it becomes private.

The total quantity of a private good in an economy is the sum of the goods being used by individuals. But for public goods, each user has access to the entire good. For example, you are protected by the entire fire department.

When economists speak of public goods, they usually mean civic goods, those goods and services typically provided by governments, such as parks, streets, and security. Many economists have thought that while private goods can be provided efficiently by a market process, collective goods cannot and require government provision by force. This argument is called "market failure." According to this argument, since all individuals have access to the entire public good, there is no way to make any individual pay for it. People will want to be "free riders."

This argument overlooks the fact that most civic goods service a particular territory. They make the area more desirable, and thus increase its land rent and land value. People located in that space must pay rent or buy land in order to live or work there. This turns the market-failure argument on its head: users are not free riders, since they pay rent; it is the landowners who can be free riders if the goods are not paid out of that rent.

The rent can be collected either by a government or by a private community such as a residential association and spent for the collective good. Civic goods then become self-financing, since the rent generated by the good is used to pay for the good. The use of rent also lets us determine the efficient amount of the good to provide. So long as each extra amount of the good increases rent more than it increases the cost, more should be provided until the marginal cost just equals the marginal rent generated.

Some collective goods are not territorial, but are excludable—those not paying for it can be excluded from using it. An example is a club which offers services only to its members. Indeed, the term "club" has become generalized in economics to mean any organization organized for some purpose. Clubs goods can be offered in exchange for membership dues, admissions, and other user fees. If a service becomes crowded, the club or government can also charge a congestion fee to encourage less usage during peak times (or a discount during non-peak times). An example is a bus or train that charges more during rush hours.

Non-excludable collective goods are those which are not territorial and are available to all who want them. An example is knowledge, once it is published. The market-failure argument is often applied to these public goods. But in fact, many such services are provided voluntarily. People contribute time and money to civic and charitable projects partly for self-centered reasons, such as to be listed as a patron, but mainly from non-mercenary reasons.

As discussed in Chapter 10, Adam Smith observed that people are also motivated by sympathy to others, to communities, and to ideas, and Henry George also discussed this desire for the well being of others and for social approval. People will contribute to a community or to some project when they have sympathy with it. This sympathy can be stimulated by social entrepreneurs who lead communities and movements.

2. PUBLIC FINANCE

Public finance is the branch of economics which is concerned with how governments raise and spend money. Its topics include an analysis of various types of taxes, government debt, budgets, and expenditures.

Taxation and public revenue

A tax is a compulsory payment to a government unrelated to any direct penalty, voluntary service, or debt. Some payments to governments have the form of a tax, as compulsory payments, but not the substance, since the payment is for a service or rent for the use of property. When an oil company pays a lease for offshore oil fields, for example, this is a rental charge for property owned by the government on behalf of the people, so it is not a tax in substance. Likewise, the collection of land rent by a community may be tax in form as a compulsory payment once the land is obtained, but not in substance, since the ownership of land is voluntary and the payment is a rent for land if one agrees it is properly owned by the community.

Taxes can be imposed on two basic types of items: property and transactions. Transaction taxes includes those on sales, value-added, income, gifts, and inheritance. The effect of imposing such arbitrary costs on transactions is to skew the prices of the items taxed, distorting the price signals of a market economy. Sales taxes make goods more expensive, labor taxes make labor more expensive, and taxes on profits make entrepreneurship and enterprise more expensive by reducing profits. Such taxes have the same effect as an increase in the cost of production due to more expensive inputs. Depending on the responsiveness of supply and demand to changes in price, transaction taxes are partly borne by workers as lower real wages, partly by enterprises as lower total profits, and partly by consumers as higher prices and a lower quantity of goods purchased. Gift taxes punish the free transfer of goods; inheritance taxes punish the preservation of family heritage and the ability to pass on an enterprise to one's children.

Taxes on income and on sales have a similar effect in reducing output, employment, and income. Taxes on wages, such as income taxes, impose a "tax wedge" on labor, making it expensive to employers while reducing the net wages of workers. This, especially combined with minimum wages, creates unemployment by making the lowest-quality labor too expensive to hire. Taxes on sales also reduce income, since the purpose of production is consumption, and if goods are taxed, purchasing power is reduced. A "value added" tax is imposed at each stage of production; for example, when trees are cut down, when lumber is cut, when furniture is made, and when it is sold, each state gets taxed according to the increase in value from one stage to the next. The result is higher prices, lower output, and lower employment.

As Henry George (1883, p. 123) stated, "We, in fact, treat the man who produces wealth, or accumulates wealth, as though he had done something which public policy calls upon us to discourage." Employment, enterprise, consumption, production, exchange—all these are social benefits, yet taxation treats these as crimes fit to be punished. "So, too, if a man saves, out taxes operate to punish him for his thrift" (p. 124).

A difference in taxing income and sales or value added is that income taxes penalize savings, while sales taxes penalize borrowing. When income taxes are applied to savings, they reduce the yield and punish the savor for postponing consumption. When people borrow funds to buy something, a sales tax is applied also to that part of the purchase paid for with borrowed funds. Suppose a car costs $20,000 and the sales tax is 5%. The buyer needs to borrow $1000 extra for the tax, and then pay interest on that $1000. Since people borrow funds and save at different stages of life, and borrowing equals savings, the macro effect of taxes on income and on sales is similar—they hurt business.

Taxes on property fall either on natural resources or on produced goods such as cars and buildings. A tax on a produced good has a similar effect to that on transactions, since a good is the product of transactions. Goods are made more expensive. But a "tax" (in form) or charge or fee on the use of natural resources, such as land, reduces its price. Since it has no cost of production, its supply curve is vertical. The demand is not affected by the charge, so it must be borne entirely by the title holder or owner. For surface land, the formula $p = r / (i+t)$ indicates that the price of land p will be reduced when the tax rate t (as a percentage of the price) is increased, r being the annual rent and i the real interest rate (see Foldvary 2006 for a detailed analysis of land value taxation or public revenue from land rent).

Whereas taxes on transactions and produced goods reduce output, a rental charge on land can increase productivity if the land was underused, being held for prestige purposes or in speculation waiting for higher prices. A pollution charge or fee is a type of rent paid for the use of land as a dump, and this charge does increase the price of goods, but this increase is really compensation for the damage caused by the pollution, so this increase is not an intervention but conforms to a market.

The taxes that most conform to markets and improve rather than decrease productivity are therefore rental charges for the use of natural resources, including surface land, underground resources such as water and minerals and oil, air rights, electro-magnetic (radio wave) frequency rents, and pollution charges.

Government budgets and deficits

Many national governments habitually spend more than they get in taxes and fees because it is politically and personally rewarding to spend money. Taxpayers don't object too much, since the repayment of the debt is pushed into the future, probably to future generations. There have been high annual deficits in the United States, with trillions of dollars in official debt and much more in unfunded liabilities such as pensions and potential insurance claims.

Ideally, a government budget should be split into two parts, one an operating budget for normal annual expenses, such as paying the salaries of the military, and the other, a capital budget for major investments in capital goods such as a highway or dam. If the capital project makes the economy more productive, then it makes economic sense to borrow the funds to create it, just as enterprises borrow funds to expand productive facilities. In that case, the debt should consist of bonds marked specifically for the project, with a maturity date when the bonds are to be paid back. The total debt would consist of such bonds, thus avoiding generalized indefinite debt.

The operations side of the budget is best funded from current-year revenues, without any debt. As Henry George (1883, p. 162) stated, "The institution of public debts ... rests upon the preposterous assumption that one generation can bind another generation." In a genuine capital budget, the debt is offset by a productive asset that is also being passed on, an asset that yields enough to pay off the debt, hence no real burden is passed on. But debt for current expenses has no corresponding asset value and return.

Of course the resources used in debt-financed operational spending are not physically taken from the future, but from the reduction in current private-sector consumption. The problem is that future persons will have their consumption reduced by the government's forcibly transferring some of their income to those who have previously lent funds to the government. It is therefore better morally and economically to reduce the current private consumption by taxation or assessment, so that present-day government-sector consumption is paid for by the present-day consumers.

There is also a public-choice aspect to a public debt. As George (1883, p. 167) realized, "A great public debt creates a great moneyed interest that wants 'strong government' and fears change." Holders of government bonds become a lobby for the preservation of that debt, as safe treasury bills and bonds become woven deep into the fabric of the financial markets.

Expenditure

Each section of a budget should include both the annual expense and the source of the revenue, so that any new project or agency is accompanied by payment.

Any voluntary association may economically spend funds according to the desires of its members and in accord with its constitution. Spending becomes a problem when the government is not a voluntary association, but is imposed without unanimous consent, at least at the constitutional level of joining a jurisdiction. When revenues are derived from site rents, we can determine the most efficient amount to spend on some collective good or service. A desired territorial good will increase the land rent of the area, so the optimal amount of the good will occur when the marginal or extra rent generated by an extra unit of the good just equals the marginal cost of the extra unit.

Many governments have found that contracting out many of its services results in lower costs than providing it directly. The reason is that competitive firms have an incentive to keep costs at a minimum, whereas with a government monopoly, the civic employees will benefit from high budgets and the government will lack the knowledge if not the incentive to keep the costs low.

Chapter 17: The National Economy

1. GROSS DOMESTIC PRODUCT

The total amount of production in an economy is called the gross domestic product, GDP. If we use the income of nationals rather than within the territory, the total is called gross national product, GNP. Some of this production goes to repair and maintain machinery and structures that depreciate; they deteriorate and wear down every year. This annual depreciation reduces the net income we get from the production, so another measurement is the net national product, or NNP, which is GNP minus depreciation. We can also compute the net domestic product, NDP. The most common measurement of national output is now the GDP.

Government's calculation of GDP leaves out some types of production, such as illegal goods and work done for oneself at home. But the GDP data also do not take into account the depletion of material resources such as oil, and the social cost of pollution.

There are many ways to divide up the GDP. One is by industry sectors, normally with three: the primary sector, made up of agriculture, forestry, fishing, and mining; the manufacturing sector, including construction; and the service sector.

The classical division was by the factors or resources that produce wealth: land, labor, and capital goods. An economy can also be divided into the three abstract types of agents: households, firms, and government. Households (in this simplified abstraction) own all the assets, the capital goods and land, and provide labor to firms; they also buy the goods produced by firms. Firms hire input factors and produce goods. Government obtains revenue from both firms and households, and provides services to both. There are two opposite flows: goods flow in one direction (such as from firms to households), while money flows in the opposite direction (from households to firms). Income is earned by households and government; the income of firms is ultimately paid to factors, to the government, and to the owners.

There are two types of expenditure categories. Income may be used for consumption or for economic investment in capital goods and human capital. Investment is the creation of capital goods. Net investment is gross investment minus depreciation. In common language, people say they invest in land or in bonds, which can yield financial returns. But in economic terminology, only the creation of new capital goods is investment. When someone buys a bond or land, money simply changes hands, since no new land is created, and a bond is simply a debt.

These categories can now be put together as follows. First, the factors of land, labor, and capital goods are hired from households by firms, which create wealth in the three sectors, primary, manufacturing, and service. This wealth goes to their owners as factor payments by firms in the form of rent, wages, and capital yields, all of which constitute income. Governments obtain some of this income either from rent or from taxes. This income is spent for consumption and investment.

2. ECONOMIC MODELS

Simple models of an economy usually involve household consumption and investment and the government sector. Waste is not usually included in these macroeconomic models. The symbol Y is usually used for national income. The most common equation is:

$Y = C + G + I$,

or income = consumption + government spending + investment.

The total output of an economy can also be abstractly formulated by an aggregate production function, with output as a function of the factors of production. This assumes, for simplicity, that all firms are identical, so that the aggregate or total production function is just the sum of the functions of the individual firms. Economists usually simplify the function with two factors, labor and capital, but it is more accurate to include land as a separate factor:

$Y = f(N, K, L)$,

where N stands for the number of workers, K for capital, and L for land.

Workers are hired until their marginal product is equal to the prevailing wage. The real wage consists of nominal wages, the money amount of wages, divided by some price index. The real wage is thus set equal to the marginal product of labor, which is the extra output generated by the aggregate production function when the number of workers increases by one (mathematically, the derivative of the function with respect to N).

In actuality, there is no single aggregate production function, since land is divided into zones of differing productivity. A more realistic production function would consist of the sum of the functions within each zone. The wage level is set at the marginal zone where land rent is zero, as described in Chapter 2.

Models also have some labor supply curve, with wages usually regarded as increasing with greater N. But in actuality, the labor supply curve can be horizontal so long as there is unemployment.

The models usually include some consumption function, where consumption depends on income, taxes, the interest rate, and other variables.

Investment is a function of the amount of capital goods, the interest rate, the depreciation rate, the number of workers, and other variables.

The above constitutes the real side of an economy, with real goods. There is also a money side, with the money supply a function of income, interest rates, and other variables, including monetary policy. In a classical model, the amount of money does not matter, since real output is determined independently of money; the price level will adjust to whatever the money supply is. In other models, especially of the Keynesian school, money does influence the real output. Both are right. In the short run, money can indeed influence output, but over the long run, inflation will simply increase prices, distorting relative prices in the process.

Chapter 18: International Trade

1. THE CASE FOR INTERNATIONAL TRADE

The principle that modern economies are based on exchange is accepted by both economists and the public, and it is generally agreed that trade within a country should not be restricted among cities, provinces, and states. But many people have a different opinion about trade among countries. What is it about a national boundary that makes it desirable to have trade barriers, aside from political reasons such as national defense? National boundaries rarely map out an area that is self-sufficient. Trade allows a nation to concentrate on producing that combination of goods for which it is most efficient.

"Gains from trade" are the additional output that takes place when parties exchange goods. There are two sources of gains from trade: one is that, among nations, differing natural resource endowments will lead to advantages in the production of certain kinds of commodities. The second source of gain stems from the decreasing cost of production that results from specialization. Resource endowments include land (including agricultural land, rainfall, minerals and oil, water, climate, and ports), labor (including skills and the wage level), and capital goods (including technology, knowledge, and historical capital such as architecture and culture).

The most obvious type of gain is an absolute advantage, which is the ability to produce a greater quantity of some product than another country, using the same inputs. Imagine that with one unit of resources, the U.S. can produce 10 units of apples and 6 units of shoes, and that with the same resources, the European Community can produce 5 units of apples and 10 units of shoes. The U.S. then has an absolute advantage in apples and the European Union has an absolute advantage in the production of shoes.

The more resources are transferred from shoes to apple production in the U.S. and vice versa in the EUROPEAN UNION, the greater will be the overall and most efficient production of both goods.

However, will trade still occur if the U.S. has an absolute advantage over the EUROPEAN UNION in the production of both apples and shoes? David Ricardo in 1817 resolved the question with the theory of comparative advantage. Suppose a lawyer can earn $100 per hour doing legal work, and can type 100 words per minute. Suppose secretaries can be hired for $10 per hour, but they can only type 50 words per minute. The lawyer has an absolute advantage in typing. Should he hire the secretary anyway? Yes, because the secretary has a relative advantage in typing. If he does his own typing, he saves $20 per hour (from two secretaries), but loses $100 in legal work, for a net loss of $80. He is better off hiring two secretaries to do what he could do in an hour. The same principle applies to trade between countries.

There can be gains from specialization and trade even when there is no absolute advantage. By concentrating in what it is best at, a country will be better off exporting that item and importing what it is relatively less efficient at. Gains can be derived from the process of specialization itself. An economy which specializes in the production of certain goods will develop economies of scale—greater efficiency with greater output, as with automobile manufacturing. Secondly, an economy will gain skill in efficiency, quality, and variety. Comparative advantage is not a given, but can be created, and lost. The theory of comparative advantage is dynamic, as both natural and created advantages change over time.

Gains from specialization depend on the "terms of trade." This concept measures the amount of imported goods that can be obtained per unit of exported goods. A rise in the price of imported goods, while that of exports remains unchanged, reduces the terms of trade. The dramatic increase in oil prices in the 1970s led to a decrease in the terms of trade for oil-importing countries. In the last few decades, some developing countries have seen the prices for their export commodities steadily decline. Markets adjust to changing terms of trade by importing less of the item increasing in price (such as conserving oil and finding substitutes) and switching from exports that lose relative value to those, such as manufactures, which are gaining in relative value.

2. FREE TRADE AND TRADE BARRIERS

Free trade is the exchange of goods without any trade barriers such as quotas and tariffs. Trade barriers consist in interference by the government to "protect" domestic industries. This trade limitation is commonly referred to as a protectionist policy. Protectionism is also called "mercantilism," from the mercantile economic system that European countries pursued from the 1500s to the 1700s, when trade was tightly regulated. Adam Smith, in The Wealth of Nations, showed how trade limitation reduces wealth, since if all countries restrict trade, the result is less wealth in each country. Yet, most governments impose restrictions on trade in an effort to "protect" domestic industries. There are political reasons for mercantilism—some industries influence the government to favor their special interest at the expense of the public well being.

The two basic types of trade limitation are tariffs and quotas. A tariff or import duty is a tax on imported goods. Tariffs raise the price of the good, reducing the quantity demanded and thus reducing the amount imported and making domestic production more profitable. An import quota is a limitation on the quantity of an import, which enables domestic producers to raise their prices. Either way, consumers are worse off, due to the higher prices and lower quantities of the goods. The ultimate quota is zero—an embargo or prohibition on the import and export of goods. For example, the United States has had an embargo on trade with Cuba. Some countries also impose a tax on exports, which by making exports more expensive reduces their production. Despite the negative effects on the economy, many less-developed countries impose taxes on foreign trade because such taxes are easier to collect than taxes on production, and such taxes enable them to avoid taxing land, which may be opposed by powerful elites.

Another option available to the government wishing to restrict imports, is to reduce the demand for the imported good. One way to do this is to legally require a percentage of domestic production in some goods. The demand for foreign goods can also be restricted by limiting the use of foreign exchange and also by manipulating currency exchange rates, making the domestic currency less valuable relative to foreign money, increasing the price of imports, reducing the quantity demanded.

All such restrictions on free trade damage the general welfare, at least in the short run. Those advocating trade barriers argue that these encourage economic development in the long run by protecting "infant industries" until they can mature and obtain more experience and a lower cost. But another way to protect such industries is with subsidies, which leave fewer distortions in the relative price structure and make the cost more explicit. More fundamentally, there is no guarantee that the protected industry will become more efficient; just the opposite can occur, as the firms rely on artificially high prices to remain inefficient. Also, trade limitation subjects the process to political influences. It is also not clear why the initial time when the industry is getting started should not be paid for by the investors rather than the taxpayers. The infant-industry argument is therefore weak at best and subject to the problem of the lack of knowledge as to whether it will succeed and to manipulation by special interests. Once an industry is given a privileged position, it becomes a special interest that will perpetually seek to preserve its privilege.

Many trade limitations, involving both subsidies and quotas, do not involve infant industries at all, but are an attempt to preserve the economic condition of an industry, such as agriculture, which cannot be sustained at current market prices. For example, the Common Agricultural Policy of the European Union costs its taxpayers many billions per year. In the European Sugar Policy, the European Community subsidizes the overproduction of beet sugar in inefficient places such as Great Britain and Portugal. Indeed, every country in the European Union is producing sugar, despite of the fact that France and Italy alone could adequately supply all of Europe's needs. The result of the EU Sugar Policy is to produce three million more tones of beet a year than Europeans can consume. The damage caused by this policy goes beyond the waste of taxpayers' money. The surplus production is dumped on the world market, reducing the price of cane sugar exported by developing countries (Rowling, 1987, p. 70).

The United States also restricts sugar imports with quotas as well as price support, further depressing world market prices. In an attempt to protect farmers from world prices, the U.S. Government sets target prices for crops and pays the difference. The U.S. government also uses quotas. Peanuts, for example, have both a quota on imports and price supports, and milk, butter, and cheese have been protected with price supports.

Trade limitations are also imposed to protect labor from lower-wage competition abroad. Manufacturing enterprise has been shifting labor-intensive production such as textiles to economies with lower labor costs, and workers in the domestic industries then lobby for trade barriers on the lower-priced imports. In the interventionist markets of today, displaced workers often have a difficult time finding other work of the same wage scale. In a free market, prosperity and the absence of a tax wedge on wages would provide a continuous demand for skilled labor, so that those who become trained in new fields or are willing to relocate to growing areas would find ready employment.

Trade barriers are defended as a superficial treatment of effects, rather than as the fundamental remedy of the cause, of low wages and unemployment. As Henry George (1886, p. 9) stated in his book *Protection or Free Trade*, "the advocates of protection ... extol the virtues of protection as furnishing employment, without asking how it comes that any one should need to be furnished with employment; they assert that protection maintains the rate of wages, without explaining what determines the rate of wages."

Advocates of trade limitation inconsistently advocate tariffs between countries but not within countries, and they do not advocate other barriers which would have the same effect. If trade barriers are beneficial, why not others? As George (1886, p. 35) put it, "Who would think of recommending a site for a proposed city or a new colony because it was very difficult to get at? Yet, if the protective theory be true, this would really be an advantage." Piracy would also be welcomed as increasing the cost of imports. Also, we regard canals, railroads, and better ships as beneficial, yet how can tariffs then be beneficial? Improved transportation reduces the cost of bringing in foreign goods, while tariffs increase the cost. "We maintain a tariff with the avowed purpose of keeping out the products of cheap foreign labor; yet machines are daily invented that produce goods cheaper than the cheapest foreign labor" (p. 36).

George also asks (p. 37), "Is there not, in the first place, an obvious absurdity in taking the nation or country as the protective unit and saying that each should have a protective tariff!" National boundaries have been changing constantly. "Political changes in no wise alter soil, climate, or industrial needs" (p. 39). If Virginia goods must be protected from those of France, why not also protect them from the imports of New York or California? If Virginia was a separate country, there would likely be such tariffs. Would it be for political or economic reasons? Aside from national defense, there is no economic difference between domestic exchange and international exchange.

To counter trade barriers and promote international trade, especially in manufactured goods, the General Agreement on Tariffs and Trade (GATT) was signed in 1947. It was then changed to the World Trade Organization, WTO. Since GATT was founded, significant reductions in tariffs have been achieved by the member states. Many developing countries which maintained protectionist policies have been liberalizing their trading policies. Regional trading blocks such as the European Community and the North American Free Trade Agreement (NAFTA) are reducing trade barriers in continental regions.

What do you think is the most valuable import into our economy? It is solar radiation from the sun. There is no cost or tariff on imported sunlight. Is that bad?

3. THE IMPACT OF TRADE ON LAND

A major problem with international trade is the unequal environmental policy among countries. For example, as U.S. companies relocate south of the border in search of cheap labor, some companies have dumped toxic waste into the Rio Grande, causing serious health and water-supply problems in the area. But such pollution is not part of "free" trade. A truly free market consists of voluntary exchanges, and dumping pollutants is not voluntary to the victims. Polluting is an act of force unless it is agreed to. The second best solution is compensation for the damage cause. Hence, in a free market, polluters must be charged for the social costs. As noted in Chapter 13, this charge is a type of rent for the use of land (including water and air as economic land) as a dump.

The problem in free trade is then to equalize such pollution charges, otherwise some countries will have an unjust advantage. Those with lower pollution charges will have lower production costs, but these are really environmental costs being imposed on others. Free trade thus requires an international agreement on common charges for environmental destruction.

A comprehensive agreement would include fees, fines, and other charges on any use and abuse of natural resources, including pollution, the destruction of wildlife, deforestation, and soil erosion.

The other impact that trade has on land is the increase in land rent and land value that accompanies an increase in productivity and investment. A substantial amount of the benefits will go to landowners. The collection of this rent by local and national communities will enable the population as a whole to benefit equally from this increase in prosperity. We can look to Great Britain for an illustration. During the days of the British Empire, the western UK ports—Bristol, Liverpool and Glasgow—were the most prosperous. After the decision to align Britain more closely with European countries, British ports on the east coast became the new centers of prosperity, with a subsequent increase in land values. The land owners of the east received a windfall from the activity of the ports. The collection of the land rent by the UK would equalize this benefit rather than letting it fall to those who did nothing to cause it.

The issue of international trade thus has an intimate connection with public revenue and environmental policy. Truly free trade requires the community collection of rent, including pollution charges, just as it requires the removal of taxes and restrictions on trade.

Chapter 19: History and Schools of Economic Thought

In studying economics, we encounter different schools of thought regarding phenomena such as business cycles, national income, markets, and international trade. Students will also encounter their names and theories. It is therefore worth while to see what these schools teach and how they are different.

1. MERCANTILISM

During the 1500s through the 1700s, the mercantilist school predominated in Europe. The main object of trade was said to be the acquisition of bullion—gold and silver—for the national treasury. Such riches would enable a country to have a strong military and also use this wealth for domestic investment. Mercantilists also promoted domestic industry with government protection and aid. To acquire precious metals, a country needed to either possess mines, as did Spain in its Latin American colonies, or to have an export surplus which would be balanced out with an importation of metals.

One problem with such a mercantilist policy is that one country's trade surplus implies deficits in other countries, so all countries cannot together succeed. As Adam Smith was to argue in his Wealth of Nations, when all countries restrict trade, the result is less wealth overall.

2. PHYSIOCRACY

In reaction to mercantilist policy, a school of though arose in France during the 1700s, the first to call themselves "economists." They called their school "physiocracy," which means "the rule of natural law." The most prominent of the Physiocratic economists was Françoise Quesnay. Physiocratic theory emphasizes free trade as removing barriers which harm consumers.

In physiocratic theory, nature provides a "net product" which is a surplus beyond the payment to labor and the provides of capital. This is equivalent to what we now recognize as land rent. Instead of taxing industry, the physiocrats theorized that the net product could be an "impôt unique" or "single tax" that could provide for all government revenue. Much of this revenue could then be invested in infrastructure and other capital investments, which would further increase productivity, increasing rent or the net product even more, thus putting into effect an upward spiral of economic development. The Physiocrats thus had the first model of the circular flow of an economy and a model of economic development which was to be successfully applied by Japan and Taiwan.

3. THE CLASSICAL SCHOOL

Also in reaction to mercantilist economics, and influenced by the physiocrats, Adam Smith in 1776 began the school which was to be called the "classical." As noted above, Smith showed how free trade would increase the "wealth of nations." His book, a major systematic treatise on economics, showed how the general welfare was increased by persons acting out of self-interest in a free market. Smith emphasized the productivity caused by a division of labor. Classical economists believed in the "labor theory of value," that the value of goods comes from the labor used to produce it, a view refuted by later economists. Also a moral philosopher, Smith's book, The Theory of Moral Sentiments, showed how people are not just self-interested but also can act out of sympathy with others or some cause.

David Ricardo in the early 1800s expanded the though of Smith to analyze the effects of growth on land rent. Population growth would push production to less productive land, thus increasing land rent while keeping wages at a subsistence level. Ricardo also furthered the theory of international trade with the concept of comparative advantage, showing how trade was mutually advantageous.

John Stuart Mill was another major classical economist as well as philosopher and the author of the famous essay On Liberty. Writing in the mid 1800s, his text was a widely used benchmark in economics. The classical school theorized that free markets provide for maximum prosperity, and that land rent is an especially suitable source of taxation. However, social problems, labor unrest, and continuing poverty raised doubts among some about the virtues of markets. Some economists, including Mill, turned to various degrees and types of socialism for remedies.

4. SOCIALIST ECONOMICS AND MARXISM

Karl Marx was a German philosopher and economist who settled in Great Britain and collaborated with Friedrich Engels in much of their work, including The Communist Manifesto. Marx's main book, Das Kapital or Capital, in three volumes, was as much a critique of so-called "capitalism" or market economies as a treatise on the socialist alternative, which was not described in much detail. Marx divided society into two main classes, capitalists who owned property and the proletariat workers.

Basing his analysis on the labor theory of value, Marx held that revenues of production belonged to labor, and the surplus value, or profits, properly belonged to workers. For that reason, and due to an army of unemployed workers which keeps wages low, capitalists exploit workers. Eventually, however, as capital goods accumulate, the rate of profit will fall, and industry will become more concentrated in ownership. Eventually, the proletariat would revolt and own the means of production, sharing the product according to need.

Modern Marxist economists follow Marx's general line of thought, with various modifications. Despite the failure of socialist systems and the theoretical criticism of Marxist thought, Marxists continue to believe that the market process is inherently flawed and needs much fixing.

5. GEOCLASSICAL ECONOMICS

Henry George was an American classical economist, but was also very critical of much of classical thought and presented alternative theories. His major work was Progress and Poverty, written in 1879. Thus he and his Georgist followers form a school of their own, which I call "geoclassical," the term "geo" standing for both George and for land. It has elements in common with both the Physiocrat and the classical school. But George rejected the classical notion of Malthus that population will tend to outrun production, and he also argued against the classical "wages fund" theory that wages are paid from some fixed amount of capital fund.

Instead, George theorized that wages are set at the margin of production, where the best free land is available, and production of better land, after paying wages and capital yields, constitutes land rent. Land rent is increased and wages lowered by land speculation, which pushes the margin to less productive land. The remedy for the resulting poverty is the collection of land rent for public revenue and the abolition of the taxation of labor and capital. This will not only increase the margin to more productive land, but also remove the stifling effects of taxing and restricting labor. George also advocated free trade just as the classicals and physiocrats did.

Hence, while socialists advocate the replacement of markets with central planning and redistribution, the geoclassical school recognizes that markets are not truly free if restricted and taxed, and it is these interventions that cause unemployment and poverty. Prosperity can be attained by removing these barriers, not erecting others.

6. THE AUSTRIAN SCHOOL

In 1871, Carl Menger, an economist in Vienna, Austria, wrote *The Principles of Economics* in reaction to German economists who based their though on historical studies, without the need for any general abstract theory and also in reaction to some classical concepts. In contrast to the classical labor theory of value, Menger recognized that value and utility are entirely subjective, independent of labor and other inputs. The value of land, labor, and capital goods are base on the values and utility people place on consumer goods.

Besides subjectivism, Menger's theory included marginal analysis, in which the value and market price of a good is based on the utility of the marginal or extra increment of the good obtained. This marginal utility diminishes with increasing amounts of the good. Trade is beneficial because people exchange goods of lower marginal utility for those of higher marginal utility. Menger also developed a theory of money based on its origin in exchangeable commodities.

This analysis began a new school of thought, called the Austrian. Other economists in the school included Böhm Bawerk, who worked out a theory of capital and interest. Ludwig von Mises also wrote on this theme, recognizing that interest rates depend on time preference (see Chapter 5). Mises' main treatise, Human Action, written in 1949, is a staunch defense of the market process. Mises and another Austrian, Friedrich von Hayek, argued against socialism, saying that economic calculation required the competitive enterprise of markets, so socialism would be ineffective.

Austrian thought emphasizes the importance of basing theory on individuals and their subjective values. Besides marginal analysis, Austrian theory emphasizes the spontaneous order of market processes, the uncertainty of the future, the importance of the heterogenous aspects of capital and money creation, and the decentralized nature of knowledge. Austrians such as Hayek have further developed the theory of capital, and modern Austrians have pioneered the theory and study of the history of free banking. Austrians also have a theory of the business cycle emphasizing the role of money creation and interest rates. Contemporary Austrians are now world-wide.

7. THE NEOCLASSICAL SCHOOL

Besides Menger, two other economists, Stanley Jevons in Great Britain and Leon Walras in France pioneered marginal utility theory and thus sparked a revolution in economic thought that converted most economists from classical to neoclassical analysis. In neoclassical thought, the value of goods derives not from labor but from their marginal utility. The classical differentiation of land and capital became blurred, as neoclassical theory became described in mathematical terms. Land became treated as part of capital.

Walras pioneered the theory of general equilibrium, with a model of an entire economy where all production is interrelated in an equilibrium setting all prices and quantities. Alfred Marshall in Great Britain developed the theory of supply and demand, including the geometrical conventions of the curves. In Sweden, Knut Wicksell, influenced also by Austrians, further developed theories of capital, interest, and public finance. Favorable to taxing land, Wicksell originated the concept of the natural rate of interest in a free market.

8. THE INSTITUTIONAL SCHOOL

While most economic theory is based on abstract supply and demand, factors, and expenditure, the institutional school points out that organizations also influence economic activity. The American economist Thorstein Veblen was a key theorist in this approach. Government, large corporations, banks, labor unions, and social organizations certainly affect the outcomes of economies, and institutionalist economics is important in the understanding of economic history and current economic life. The theory of institutions is also part of basic economic theory. Both the Austrian and geoclassical schools have included institutional concepts in their theories, including the role of central banks in Austrian monetary theory and the role of land tenure in geoclassical theory.

9. THE INTERVENTIONIST SCHOOL AND KEYNESIANISM

During the great world-wide depression of the 1930s, many neo-classical economists came to doubt the full-employment claims of neo-classical macroeconomic theory, although Austrians and geoclassical economists recognized that the economies of the early 20th century had many interventions which had led to the depression. John Maynard Keynes in Great Britain published the book The General Theory of Employment, Interest and Money in 1936, claiming to overturn many neo-classical concepts, although microeconomic neoclassical theory was not questioned.

Keynes argued that wages would not automatically or swiftly adjust to a lower supply/demand juncture, but can remain stuck at a high level, reducing the demand for labor and creating unemployment. Also, Keynes disagreed with the classical and neoclassical concept that investment increases with lower interest rates. To Keynesians, markets do not necessarily work well, and they are not always self-correcting when unemployment rises and output declines. Government intervention is needed to boost demand. Whereas classical theory states that the supply side determines output, since factors are paid the full amount of the product, and since prices adjust to equilibrate supply and demand, Keynesian interventionists claim that prices and wages don't in fact adjust, and that in a money economy, the total demand for products can be insufficient, since people don't necessarily spend enough.

Keynesian policy thus emphasizes increasing demand during a depression by increasing the money supply, by increasing government spending, raising the money supply, and reducing taxes to increase private spending. During a boom, the government can reverse these policies to reduce inflation. Interventionists have restored some mercantilist policies, some arguing for protectionist measures.

Critics of such interventionist policies point out that the interventions, first of all, do not necessarily work in the long run. Inflating the money supply eventually raises prices and stops raising output, aside from distorting prices and production. Also, these policies attempt to treat the effects of economic problems without analyzing the root causes, which turn out to be interventions rather than the market process itself.

In response to these critiques, a New-Keynesian school has developed, with more sophisticated theories of how markets fail and how intervention can correct them, so the debate continues.

10. THE NEW-CLASSICAL MACROECONOMIC SCHOOL

In reaction to interventionists, especially in money and banking, the monetarist school restored the classical theory of money that emphasizes the role of the quantity of money. High money expansion in the long run leads to inflation rather than increasing output. A key monetarist has been Milton Friedman in the United States. Monetarists point out that government does not have the knowledge to respond to every twist and turn in the economy, so instead of discretionary policy, it is better to have some rule that will be followed by central banks. Monetarism is not a complete macroeconomic theory, but is a school within macroeconomics, especially for monetary economics.

More comprehensively, some economists have argued against intervention as the "new classical" school. A key concept in this school is that of "rational expectations," which states that people create judgments about future economic variables such as inflation using past information and some model or theory of the economy, by which they will avoid systematic mistakes. The New-Keynesian school has accepted rational expectations, so it is not an exclusively new-classical principle, but it is used to rebut some interventionist policies, since the new-classicalists state that people will recognize and respond to expected policy.

11. THE POST-KEYNESIAN SCHOOL

A new macroeconomic school of thought based on Keynesian thought, expanded by the work of the Polish economist Michael Kalecki, has been called "post-Keynesian." They follow Keynesians in believing that markets don't always clear and that individuals don't always perceive the correct market signals. They also have adopted some institutionalist thought and a Marxist emphasis on the different economic classes, the workers and capitalists. Post-Keynesian thought has also been influenced by the work of the Italian-British economist, Piero Sraffa, who restored some Ricardian classical theory, where prices are determined by the costs of production.

12. FOUNDATIONAL ECONOMICS

The foundational school of economics encompasses all economic theory, micro, macro, and institutional. It seeks a comprehensive theory of economics, synthesizing the thought of all other schools in an integrated, systematic way, with a foundational based on a set of axiomatic propositions that apply to all people, times, and places. Pure theory is derived from these propositions using deductive logic. Specific theory about particular events, cultures, and economies is based on pure theory and the institutions and facts about the particular phenomena, derived using hypotheses tested by data as well as deductively. The foundational school integrates moral and economic concepts, since it recognizes that pure markets follow moral rules.

The macroeconomic model is that of a pure market economy on which interventions are imposed. Pure markets work well, providing for prosperity and full employment. In accord with the physiocratic and geoclassical schools, foundational economics agrees that land rent is the efficient source of revenue for public goods and services. In accord with classical theory, it agrees with the principles of free trade. Its trade theory combines geoclassical and Austrian elements for an integrated theory with real and monetary aspects. It also accepts the Austrian theory of interest rates based on time preference and its theory of banking.

Foundational theory encompasses neoclassical marginal analysis and price theory, but retains the classical differentiation of the three factors of production. Socialist and interventionist views are not accepted, since these are flawed or lacking axiomatic foundations.

Foundational economics is open to theory from any school or approach so long as its pure theory can be derived from the axiomatic propositions or has specific theory founded on pure theory. It can therefore potentially create a synthesis from the other schools as a comprehensive and unified theory of economics.

CONCLUSION

Most economists today are neoclassical in micro-economics and interventionist or monetarist/new-classical in macroeconomics. This author and text are foundational, drawing much from geoclassical, Austrian, and neoclassical theory. Which school do you find makes the most sense?

Chapter 20: The Law of Human Progress

1. SOCIAL PROGRESS AND DECLINE

In the final "book" in *Progress and Poverty* (p. 475), Henry George steps back from economics to survey the human condition, and asks: "What is the law of human progress?"

Is there some "great law under which human development goes on"? Conventional economics textbooks do not address this question at all. But, as George realized, it is an important issue which puts economics in the greater context of human progress, both material and cultural.

We know from history that human beings are progressive. Whereas most animals continue the same pattern of life from one generation to another, human beings pattern their lives from their cultures, which do evolve. Sometimes, cultures devolve—knowledge gets lost, conditions worsen. Is there some principle by which we can say, this favors improvement, and that does not?

George dismisses the view that human social evolution follows the same methods as biological natural selection—that in the struggle for existence, the fittest races or nationalities survive and propagate. Similarly, some have said that the individuals with the greatest ability will live and propagate, while those with inferior abilities will not. However, the hereditary survival of superior characteristics, which does apply in biological evolution, does not explain human progress.

It is often the poor who have the greatest number of children. George also points to "an enormous fact—the fixed, petrified civilizations" (p. 481). Many societies have not progressed. The proposition that superior human nationalities or families will continuously progress is refuted by the periods of progression and periods of stagnation and retrogression in civilizations such as the Chinese, the Mayan Indians, and the ancient Egyptians.

The stagnation and decline of civilizations is not an exception or isolated cases—"it is the universal rule. Every civilization that the world has seen has had its period of vigorous growth, of arrest and stagnation; its decline and fall" (p. 484). Our own civilization is still young. That we have soared high "would prove nothing as to its permanence and future advance, unless it be shown that it is superior in those things which caused the ultimate failure of its predecessors" (pp. 484–5). If social progress were due to natural selection, "the general rule would be that progress would be continuous" (p. 485), but "The earth is the tomb of the dead empires" (p. 485).

Progress itself generates its own decline, under certain conditions: "that what has destroyed all previous civilizations has been the conditions produced by the growth of civilization itself" (p. 488).

2. WHAT CAUSES PROGRESS

It is now recognized, as George realized, that a national character is determined by society's "traditions, beliefs, customs, laws, habits, and associations" (p. 494). "This is the matrix in which mind unfolds and from which it takes its stamp" (p. 504). "Human progress goes on as the advances made by one generation are in this way secured as the common property of the next, and made the starting point for many new advances" (p. 505).

The origin of all human action is in the motivations of individual human beings. All economics is ultimately based on individual human action in the context of the natural environment and of culture. And as George stated (p. 506), "The incentives to progress are the desires inherent in human nature—the desire to gratify the wants of the animal nature, the wants of the intellectual nature, and the wants of the sympathetic nature." These desires, especially the latter two, can never be fully satisfied.

"Mind is the instrument by which man advances." "Mental power" is the "motor of progress … the extension of knowledge, the improvement of methods, and the betterment of social conditions" (p. 507). Mental power is limited, and it can either be devoted to progress or to "nonprogressive" purposes such as physical and social maintenance and conflict, such as war, crime, lawsuits, domestic struggles, and defenses against these. War "can aid progress only when it prevents further war or breaks down antisocial barriers which are themselves passive war" (p. 525).

Since isolated people have less ability to propagate progress, "association is the first essential of progress." The association of people in communities "permits the division of labor and all the economies which come with the co-operation of increased numbers … Improvement becomes possible as men come together in peaceful association, and the wider and closer the association, the greater the possibilities of improvement (p. 508).

George recognized that "commerce, which is in itself a form of association or co-operation, operates to promote civilization, not only directly, but by building up interests which are opposed to warfare, and dispelling the ignorance which is the fertile mother of prejudices and animosities" (p. 512).

Since conflict draws time and energy away from progressive pursuits, a peaceful community will make more progress than one in conflict, and although conflict can generate improvements in the art of war, these improvements are potentially dangerous to civilization and progress. Conflict includes "internal resistances … which can alone explain how a civilization once fairly started should either come of itself to a halt or be destroyed by barbarians" (p. 513). George notes that conflict "becomes greater or less as the moral law which accords to each an equality of rights is ignored or is recognized." Therefore, "equality (or justice) is the second essential of progress." Justice—"the recognition of the moral law—prevents the dissipation of this power in fruitless struggles" (p. 508).

"Thus association in equality is the law of progress." We have the most progress when we co-operate in a community where equal liberty is recognized and protected. "Here is the law of progress, which will explain all diversities, all advances, all halts, and retrogression" (p. 508). Voluntary cooperation increases progress, while conflict reduces it. Liberty or "freedom, the synonym for equality, is … the stimulus and condition of progress." As liberty and justice are preserved, civilization advances, and as they are lacking, an advancing civilization will "come to a halt and recede" (p. 525).

3. THE DECLINE AND FALL OF CIVILIZATIONS

As a society advances in wealth, knowledge, and complexity, as labor becomes more specialized, there is, George observed, a tendency towards greater inequality if there are no changes in the social structure to counter it. Over time, "the garment of laws, customs, and political institutions … is constantly tending to become too tight as the society develops." Man (i.e. humanity) "threads a labyrinth, in which, if he keeps straight ahead, he will infallibly lose his way" (1879, p. 514).

The main political institution that fosters inequality is a governing monopoly. George noted that one effect of greater and more complex association "is to give rise to a collective power which is distinguishable from the sum of individual powers" (p. 515). Even if elected, if the ruling group has a perpetual monopoly on power, it will tend to be used to perpetuate its power and that of the most powerful interests. The law will reinforce unjust customs, and such customs will be perpetuated by the force of law. Ethnic segregation and discrimination is a prime example. The other institution that creates inequality is the unequal ownership of natural resources. Wages are also unequal, but the concentrated ownership of land creates more extreme inequalities that persist over generations as the land is passed on, whereas much of the inequality of wages is dissipated in one generation by high consumption.

George recognized two elements of human nature that help foster the tendency towards greater inequality. The first is habit. Customs and laws tend to be perpetuated "long after they have lost their original usefulness." The other aspect of human nature is the capacity for "moral deterioration." If change is gradual, people can get used to conditions and modes of thought that would have originally been deemed to be immoral (p. 515).

Given a monopolist authority, "as society grows, the disposition to continue previous social adjustments tends to lodge this collective power, as it arises, in the hands of a portion of the community; and this unequal distribution of the wealth and power gained as society advances tends to produce greater inequality, since aggression grows by what it feeds on, and the idea of justice is blurred by the habitual toleration of injustice" (p. 516).

In this way, a patriarchal organization develops into an absolute monarchy, a war chief becomes a despot, a priest becomes a god, as power becomes extended and exalted.

The unequal ownership of land creates economic inequalities that become also political inequalities. George notes that at first, people perceive that land is common property. Later, the idea of personal and movable property becomes transferred to land. The private ownership of the yield of the land, as opposed the marginal product of labor and capital goods, may help secure possession when the population is low, but as it becomes dense, it fosters the stratification of society into landlords and tenants.

Conquest by war is a major origin of the concentration of land and political power (p. 518). The conquerors become a dominant class, and the original inhabitants become slaves, serfs, or impoverished tenants, as the American Indians did in Latin America. Centuries later, the descendants of the conquerors claim a historical right to the land, as did the Europeans in America and South Africa.

By these methods, inequality becomes established. Social, economic, and political inequality "makes intelligible all the phenomena of petrification and retrogression," which "tends to check, and finally to counterbalance, the force by which improvements are made and society advances" (p. 518).

Power is expended in maintaining the wealth of the ruling elite and in warfare rather than for progress. Such an economy may build great statues and structures, "but it will be monuments of ruthless pride" (p. 519). The society becomes rigidified. "The same causes which tended to produce the hereditary king and hereditary priest would tend to produce the hereditary artisan and laborer, and to separate society into castes" (p. 520).

Great civilizations decay from within. "The barbarism which overwhelmed Rome came not from without, but from within. It was the necessary product of the system which had substituted slaves and coloni for the independent husbandmen of Italy, and carved the provinces into estates of senatorial families" (p. 522).

George notes that our own civilization may decline as well, and that the seeds of the decline are already planted. As discussed in Chapter 15, democracy by itself cannot avoid a decline. Most would have scoffed at this notion in George's day, but already at the close of the 20th century, the decline of Western civilization does not seem so far fetched, even as its institutions and culture triumph world-wide. Income for many workers has leveled out, government becomes an ever larger force in our lives, and violent crime reaches new heights in lives taken and loot stolen and new depths in attacks ever more vicious and widespread. Poverty and homelessness persist, workers fear for their jobs, education degenerates in schools infested by violence, much of our youth sees no future and escapes reality in drugs, while enterprise becomes ever more stifled in regulations, laws, taxes, and lawsuits. Technology still advances, and offers some hope of liberation, but government and terrorists can also use technology to wreak havoc.

The same cause which led to the downfall of previous civilizations is operating now in our own. George warns that not only are the principles of a pure market economy just and wealth-enhancing, but the failure to follow them is likely to lead to ruin: "if this is not done, progress must turn to decadence, and modern civilization decline to barbarism, as have all previous civilizations" (p. 528).

What are the indications of increasing barbarism? "One of the characteristics of barbarism is the low regard for the rights of person and of property" (p. 535). Another, as discussed Chapter 15, is the degeneration of government: "the growth of a sentiment which either doubts the existence of an honest man in public office or looks on him as a fool for not seizing his opportunities. That is to say, the people themselves are becoming corrupted … Strong, unscrupulous men, rising up upon occasion, will become the exponents of blind popular desires or fierce popular passions, and dash aside forms that have lost their vitality" (p. 537).

"Whence shall come the new barbarians? Go through the squalid quarters of great cities, and you may see, even now, their gathering hordes!" (p. 538).

George foresaw barbarism in Europe. "What shall we say of Europe, where the dams of ancient law and custom pen up the swilling waters and standing armies weigh down the safety valves, though year by year the fires grow hotter underneath? Europe tends to republicanism under conditions that will not admit of true republicanism" (p. 538). The horrors of the two world wars testify to the accuracy of his vision. The same warning can be applied to Eastern Europe and the republics of the former Soviet Union today.

Social decay is gradual, so that it may not be noticed for a long time, "though knowledge yet increases and invention marches on, and new states are being settled, and cities still expand, yet civilization has begun to wane when, in proportion to population, we must build more and more prisons, more and more almshouses, more and more insane asylums. It is not from top to bottom that societies die; it is from bottom to top" (p. 542).

4.THE UNITY OF MORAL, SOCIAL, AND ECONOMIC PRINCIPLES

The law of human progress which Henry George developed reveals the unity of moral, social and economic principles. The social law by which civilization progresses is consistent with the moral law mandating liberty and equality and the economic principle that the equal ownership of land rent, used for public goods, and free individual ownership of labor and capital goods, promotes the most prosperity. The denial of liberty and the equality of land is morally wrong, reduces prosperity, and eventually leads to the downfall of a once great civilization.

The principles of ethics, economics, and governance analyzed in this book demonstrate, as George (p. 544) stated, that "these evils are not imposed by natural laws; that they spring solely from social maladjustments which ignore natural laws, and that in removing their cause we shall be giving an enormous impetus to progress."

The distinction between form and substance, discussed in Chapter 15 in relation to democracy, applies to liberty as well. As George declared, "We honor Liberty in name and in form. We set up her statues and sound her praises. But we have not fully trusted her. And with our growth so grow her demands. She will have no half service!

"Liberty! it is a word to conjure with, not to vex the ear in empty boastings. For Liberty means Justice, and Justice is the natural law" (p. 546).

We have not yet seen the real grandeur of liberty. George, in his "Ode to Liberty," declares (p. 548): "Either we must wholly accept her or she will not stay. It is not enough that men should vote; it is not enough that they should be theoretically equal before the law. They must have liberty to avail themselves of the opportunities and means of life; they must stand on equal terms with reference to the bounty of nature. Either this, or Liberty withdraws her light! Either this, or darkness comes on, and the very forces that progress has evolved turn to powers that work destruction. This is the universal law. This is the lesson of the centuries. Unless its foundations be laid in justice the social structure cannot stand."

"We cannot go on permitting men to vote and forcing them to tramp. We cannot go on educating boys and girls in our public schools and then refusing them the right to earn an honest living. We cannot go on prating of the inalienable rights of man and then denying the inalienable right to the bounty of the Creator. Even now, in old bottles the new wine begins to ferment, and elemental forces gather for the strife!

"But if, while there is still yet time, we turn to Justice and obey her, if we trust Liberty and follow her, the dangers that now threaten must disappear, the forces that now menace will turn to agencies of elevation." But "With want destroyed; with greed changed to noble passions; with the fraternity that is born of equality taking the place of the jealousy and fear that now array men against each other; with mental power loosed by conditions that give to the humblest comfort and leisure; and who shall measure the heights to which our civilization may soar? (p. 552).

These are the principles of the science of economics, interlinked with those of the universal ethic and those of sound governance. As George recognized, "economic law and moral law are essentially one" (p. 560). The basic principles of this law are: That there is a rational ethic, a natural moral law, stemming from our equal and independent natures, whose basic rules are that evil acts are those which coercively harm others, and goods acts are welcomed benefits to others, all other acts being neutral. That a proper government at the highest, constitutional, level is the implementation of this ethic, recognizing the political sovereignty of each individual and the equality of human beings with respect to one another and with respect to our natural environment. That economic prosperity is realized when no costs and restrictions are imposed on labor and enterprise, the creation of wealth, so long as the social costs of environmental destruction are compensated for and so long as members of communities as equal co-owners share the yields of land, its rent, which can be applied to their collective services.

These are the main lessons of ethics, of political science, and of economic science. As George said, "What oppresses the masses is their own ignorance, their own short-sighted selfishness" (1883, p. 242).

Education is the antidote to ignorance, and when people become more enlightened, sympathy for a cause can replace apathy. "Whoever becomes imbued with a noble idea kindles a flame from which other torches are lit, and influences those with whom he comes in contact, be they few or many. How far that influence, thus perpetuated, may extent, it is not given to him here to see" (p. 243).

What can individuals and groups do to promote progress? Too often, organizations and movements promoting liberty, environmental protection, equal treatment, the elimination of cruelty, charity for the poor, peace, and many other causes do good work in treating effects, but don't take the time to dig deeper into the fundamental origins of the problems they deal with.

They could do better work by promoting remedies that eliminate the cause of the problems while at the same time helping to relieve distress. As George (p. 242) said, "Until there be correct thought, there cannot be right action; and when there is correct thought, right action will follow." The aim of this book is to have contributed at least to providing some of that "correct thought."

References

Atkinson, Anthony B., and Stiglitz, Joseph E. 1987. *Lectures on Public Economics.* London: McGraw-Hill.

Body, Richard. 1991. "Protectionism, Rent and the Dynamics of Agricultural Degradation." In *Now the Synthesis.* London: Shepheard-Walwyn. P. 209.

Buchanan, James. 1969 [1978]. *Cost and Choice.* Chicago: University of Chicago Press.

Churchill, Winston. 1917. "On Human Rights." Speech in the House of Commons and at the King's Theatre in Edinburgh.

East, L.R. 1945. *The Financing of Developmental Works.* Melbourne, Victoria: Melbourne University Press.

Fisher, Irving. 1930. [1986]. *The Theory of Interest.* Fairfield, NJ: Augustus M. Kelly.

Foldvary, Fred. 1980. *The Soul of Liberty.* San Francisco: The Gutenberg Press.

Foldvary, Fred. 1993. "On Monopoly Rent: Comment." *Land Economics* 69, 1 (February).

Foldvary, Fred. 1994. *Public Goods and Private Communities.* Aldershot, UK: Edward Elgar Publishing.

Foldvary, Fred. 1997. "The Business Cycle: A Georgist-Austrian Synthesis." *American Journal of Economics and Sociology* 56 (4) (October): 521–41

Foldvary, Fred. 1998. "Ignorance, Apathy, and Greed." *The Progress Report.*
<http://www.progress.org/fold21.htm>

Foldvary, Fred. 2006. *The Ultimate Tax Reform: Public Revenue from Land Rent.* Santa
Clara, Civil Society Institute. <http://www.foldvary.net/works/policystudy.pdf>

Foldvary, Fred. 2007. *The Depression of 2008.* Berkeley: The Gutenberg Press

George, Henry. 1879 [1975]. *Progress and Poverty.* New York: Robert Schalkenbach Foundation.

George, Henry. 1883 [1966]. *Social Problems.* New York: Robert Schalkenbach Foundation.

George, Henry. 1886 [1980]. *Protection or Free Trade.* New York: Rorbert Schalkenbach Foundation.

George, Henry. 1897 [1968]. *The Science of Political Economy.* New York: Robert Schalkenbach Foundation.

Hammond, J.L. and Hammond, Barbara. 1948. *The Village Laborer* (Vol.1). Guild Books.

Harrison, Fred. 1983. *The Power in the Land.* New York: Universe Books.

Hayek, Friedrich A. 1933 [1966]. *Monetary Theory and the Trade Cycle.* New York: Augustus M. Kelly.

Lester, W.R. 1936. *Unemployment and the Land.* London: The United Committee for the Taxation of Land Values.

Lloyds Bank Economic Bulletin. May 1992.

Marx, Karl. [1973]. *Grundrisse.* Trans. Martin Nicolus. Harmondsworth: Pelican Books.

McConnel, J.W. 1980. *The Ideas of the Great Economists.* Second edition. New York: Barnes and Noble Books.

Menger, Carl. 1871 [1976]. *Principles of Economics.* New York: New York University Press.

Mises, Ludwig von. 1949 [1963]. *Human Action.* New Haven: Yale University Press.

Norberg, Johan. 2009. *Financial Fiasco: How America's Infatuation with Homeownership and Easy Money Created the Economic Crisis.* Washington DC: Cato Institute.

Rowling, Nick. 1987. *Commodities: How the World Was Taken To Market.* London: Free Association Books.

Selgin, George. 1988. *The Theory of Free Banking.* Totowa: Rowman & Littlefield.

Smith, Adam. 1776 [1976]. *The Wealth of Nations.* Ed. Edwin Canaan. Chicago: University of Chicago Press.

Smith, Adam. 1790 [1982]. *The Theory of Moral Sentiments.* Indianapolis: Liberty Classics.

South Australian Commissioners. 1836. Report. England, June 24, 1836.

Todaro, Michael P. 1994. *Economic Development.* New York: Longman.

Vickrey, William. 1990. "Rent and the Provision of Social Services."

Vickrey, William. 1991. "Site value Taxes and Public Services." Lecture at St. John's University, Oct 17, 1991.

Wakefield, E. n.d. *England and America*, Vol. 2.

Wieser, Friedrich von. 1927 [1967]. *Social Economics.* Trans. A. Ford Hinrichs. New York: Augustus M. Kelley Publishers.

Whittaker, Alan. *Enslaved Children.* Report by Anti-Slavery International, 180 Brixton Road, London SW9 6AT, U.K.

Printed by Libri Plureos GmbH in Hamburg,
Germany

9 781609 279400